Henry James: The Early Novels

Twayne's United States Authors Series

David J. Nordloh, Editor
Indiana University, Bloomington

TUSAS 440

HENRY JAMES
(1843–1916)
Photograph by Notman

Henry James: The Early Novels

By Robert Emmet Long

Twayne Publishers • *Boston*

813.4
J24

Henry James: The Early Novels

Robert Emmet Long

10-87 Publ 2200
Copyright © 1983 by G. K. Hall & Company
All Rights Reserved
Published by Twayne Publishers
A Division of G. K. Hall & Company
70 Lincoln Street
Boston, Massachusetts 02111

Book Production by Marne B. Sultz
Book Design by Barbara Anderson

Printed on permanent/durable acid-free
paper and bound in the United States of
America.

Library of Congress Cataloging in Publication Data

Long, Robert Emmet.
   Henry James, the early novels.

   (Twayne's United States authors series;
TUSAS 440)
   Bibliography p. 181
   Includes index.
   1. James, Henry, 1843-1916
—Criticism and interpretation.
I. Title. II. Series.
PS2124.L62   1983   8'13'.4   82-18721
ISBN 0-8057-7379-7

For John W. Crowley

Contents

About the Author

Robert Emmet Long received his B.A. and Ph.D. from Columbia University, and has taught in the English departments of the State University of New York and Queens College (of the City University of New York). He is the author of *The Achieving of "The Great Gatsby": F. Scott Fitzgerald, 1920–1925* (1979) and *The Great Succession: Henry James and the Legacy of Hawthorne* (1979), and of over two hundred essays and reviews. His essays have appeared in many of the best-known scholarly journals, and his reviews in a variety of journals and national magazines, such as the *Saturday Review*, the *Nation*, and *Commonweal*.

Preface

This study of James's earlier novels would seem to come at a good time. The James revival has now been underway for approximately forty years, and so many books and articles have been published on James that a reader interested in his novels may well be bewildered by the sheer volume of secondary literature. What he might like to have at the present time is a single volume devoted to the earlier novels that consolidates this scholarship and brings the novels themselves into clear focus—the objectives of this study. The preparation of the book has involved reading nearly everything that has been published in English on the earlier novels, but its emphasis is on the novels themselves and the major patterns of James's development as a novelist from the beginning to *The Bostonians*. The book ends with *The Bostonians* because that novel is traditionally regarded as the culminating work of the first phase of James's career, the point at which he took up permanent residence abroad, where the later novels are set.

The book is intended for an audience of both general readers and American literature specialists. It makes the earlier novels immediately accessible to those who are not necessarily initiated into James's fiction; but it also has in mind an audience of students and scholars, for whom it offers original readings and observations, rather than a summary of what has already been said. The chapters that follow give particular stress to the evolution of the novels and the ways in which they relate, sometimes unexpectedly, to each other. Character conceptions and themes are traced from James's apprenticeship novel to the novels of his full maturity in the 1880s to reveal the steady unfolding and expansion of his vision. Certain aspects of the novels are given particular attention—James's use of both realistic and romance modes; his use of inner and outer plots, and of character doubles; his overriding concern throughout the novels with the problem of the "self."

As to the format of the book, each of the main chapters is broken down into topic sections, with introductory portions dealing with background information. In the background sections, all of the most recent information about James's circumstances at the time of the writing of the novel being discussed is provided concisely, and in such a way as to reveal the relationship between his life at the time and the novel he wrote. Relevant textual information is also given—where and when the novel was serialized; where and when it was published in book form; what the contemporary reception of the work was; when the novel was revised (whether once or more than once) and what the nature of the revision was. The sections on "source and influence" consolidate everything presently available on the subject, clearing away distractions and focusing upon essentials. The main part of each chapter is always the critical interpretation; but the background information provided is a special feature that makes the book valuable for reference; and its usefulness in this respect is increased by an annotated, up-to-date bibliography of critical studies that are concerned most directly with the earlier novels. One additional feature of the book adds to its usefulness for reference and research. The first footnote entry for each of James's titles details the previous scholarship on that specific work published since the James revival—broken down into books, sections of books, and articles. This comprehensive yet concise coverage of the earlier novels makes the book unlike any previous one published on James.

In the preparation of the book, I have been fortunate to have had Leon Edel's multivolumed biography of James, bibliography of his writings, and edition of his letters to draw on for factual information. I am indebted, for the use of their research facilities, to the Ernest Stevenson Bird Library at Syracuse University; and to the Penfield Library, at the State University of New York at Oswego, and particularly to Mr. George Scheck and the inter-

Preface

library loan staff. I would also like to express my gratitude to David Nordloh for his advice concerning technical aspects of the book, and to John Crowley for reading the manuscript. My gratitude to Carolyn is greatest of all; it is literally too large to acknowledge.

Robert Emmet Long

Chronology

1843	Henry James, Jr., born at 2 Washington Place, New York City, on April 15; second of five children of Henry James, Sr., and Mary Walsh James.
1843–1845	James family in England and Europe.
1845–1855	Family lives in New York City, chiefly at 58 West Fourteenth Street.
1855–1858	James attends various schools in Geneva, London, Paris, and Boulogne-sur-Mer. Summer, 1858, at Newport, Rhode Island, where he enjoys friendship of Thomas Sergeant Perry and John La Farge.
1859–1860	Autumn, 1859, attends schools in Geneva and Bonn.
1860–1862	Family returns to Newport; in autumn 1861, James suffers back injury, or "obscure hurt."
1862–1863	Enrolls at Harvard Law School, but chiefly pursues his private reading.
1864	Publishes first story (unsigned), "A Tragedy of Error"; and first review, in the North American Review.
1865	First signed story, "The Story of a Year," in the *Atlantic*, and a review in the first issue of the *Nation*.
1866–1868	Moves with family to Quincy Street, Cambridge, 1866, where he makes acquaintance of W. D. Howells. Begins to publish reviews in the *Atlantic*, the *North American Review*, and the *Nation*. Early stories begin to appear in magazines.
1869–1870	Travels to England, France, Switzerland, and Italy,

for his "Grand Tour." March, 1870, receives news of Minny Temple's death; April, returns to America.

1871   Publishes *Watch and Ward* in the *Atlantic* (March–April); and "A Passionate Pilgrim," also in the *Atlantic* (August–December). Summer trip to Saratoga, Newport, Niagara, and Quebec, to write travel sketches for the *Nation*.

1872–1874   Travels abroad, beginning summer, 1872. Spends winter of 1872–73 in Rome; summer, 1873, in Switzerland and Germany; winter 1873–74 in Florence and Rome. Writes European travel pieces for the *Nation*, tales of Americans abroad, and begins *Roderick Hudson*. Returns to America in autumn, 1874.

1875   Spends six months in New York City, then moves to Cambridge. *A Passionate Pilgrim, and Other Tales*, and *Transatlantic Sketches* (first books). *Roderick Hudson* serialized in the *Atlantic* (January–December). Arranges to write European letters for the *New York Tribune*. November, moves to Paris.

1876   Meets Turgenev, who introduces him to Flaubert and his circle—Maupassant, Daudet, the Goncourts, and Zola. December, leaves Paris to live in London. *Roderick Hudson* published in book form; *The American* serialized in the *Atlantic* (June, 1876–May, 1877).

1877   Book publication of *The American.*

1878   *Watch and Ward*, revised, published in book form. *French Poets and Novelists* and *The Europeans* published. *Daisy Miller* serialized in the *Cornhill Magazine.*

1879   The year of James's "conquest of London." English editions of *Roderick Hudson, The American, The Madonna of the Future, Daisy Miller,* and *Hawthorne.*

1880   Spends winter in Italy. Publishes *Confidence, The Diary of a Man of Fifty* (stories), and *A Bundle of Letters* (stories). *Washington Square* serialized jointly in the *Cornhill Magazine* and *Harper's*, summer through autumn, and published in book form in December.

1881   Spends spring and early summer in Italy; October, returns to Boston. English edition of *Washington Square. The Portrait of a Lady* serialized jointly in *Macmillan's Magazine* and the *Atlantic*, autumn, 1880–autumn, 1881.

1882   December, 1881–January, 1882, in New York and Washington, D.C. Mother dies in late January before he can reach Cambridge. May, sails for England. Autumn, "little tour in France." December, notified that his father is dying, and returns to America. December 20, father dies before James's arrival home.

1883   August, returns to London; does not visit America again for twenty years. *The Seige of London* (stories), *Portraits of Places* (travel pieces), and fourteen-volume Collective Edition of his works.

1884   February, visits Paris and renews acquaintance of Daudet, Zola, and Edmond de Goncourt. "The Art of Fiction" in *Longman's Magazine* (September). *A Little Tour in France* and *Tales of Three Cities* (stories).

1885   *The Author of "Beltraffio"* (stories) and *Stories Revived*, 3 volumes. *The Bostonians* serialized in *Century* Magazine, February, 1885–February, 1886. *The Princess Casamassima* serialized in the *Atlantic*, September, 1885–October, 1886.

1886   Book publication of *The Bostonians* (February) and *The Princess Casamassima* (October), which have poor reception and sales, and mark turning point in James's career. Spends remainder of life in England.

1916 Dies in London on February 28.

Chapter One

Introduction: The Early Years

In his long and immensely productive career, Henry James altered the nature of modern fiction. No American novelist before him had ever brought such steady, disciplined, and tireless application of will to the vocation of literature. But in his family background was a man whose force of will was also notable. The first William James, founder of the family, was an Irish Protestant who, with Bible in hand, had immigrated to America from County Cavan shortly after the Revolution. Possessing only a very small amount of money, he went to work in a tobacco store in New York City; and within two years, opened his own business, and quickly began to acquire land and property in New York, Albany, and Syracuse. He became a founder and director of banks, a trustee of Union College in Schenectady, and was principal speaker at the opening of the Erie Canal. At the time of his death in 1832, he was estimated to be the second wealthiest man in New York State, leaving a fortune of three million dollars to his widow and eleven surviving children.

William James was twice a widower when he married Catherine Barber who, between 1805 and 1828, bore him seven sons and three daughters, the fourth of these being Henry James, Sr.[1] Although born into fortunate circumstances, Henry, Sr., suffered two misfortunes in his youth. The first was the amputation of his leg, when, aged thirteen, he was seriously burned while attempting to put out a stable fire. The second was his exposure to his father's stern Presbyterianism, which so oppressed him as a youth that he spent the remainder of his life attempting to formulate a religious view of life to take its place. In his college years, James, Sr., drew on his father's credit for creature comforts ("segars and oysters"), and ran away from home to Boston, thus causing his father to regard him as a young man already on his way to ruin. When William James died in 1832, two years after his son's graduation from Union College, James, Sr., was accordingly left only a small annuity in his will. The will, however, was broken by the heirs, and James, Sr., as his share, received real estate holdings in Syracuse yielding him $10,000 a year, enough to leave him "leisured for life." Uncertain of a career, he entered Princeton Theological Seminary, only to abandon his studies two and a half years later and settle in New York. It was there, in 1840, that he met and married Mary Robertson Walsh, sister of a seminary classmate and member of a well-to-do family of Scotch-Irish extraction. Thereafter, devoting himself to what seemed to him the great questions of religion and humanity, he lived without a formal profession. His occupation largely was to be the patriarch of the James family, the father of William and Henry James—a brilliant psychologist and a great novelist. William,[2] the eldest of the children, was born in New York City, in January, 1842; Henry was born over a year later, on April 15, 1843, at the family home, at No. 21 Washington Place.

By the time of William's birth, James, Sr., had already made the acquaintance of Emerson, and at his home in New York received his ambassadors from Boston and Concord. In the America of the 1840s, Transcendentalism was at high noon, and James, Sr., shared in the restless, questing spirit of that time. Voyaging to England and settling at Windsor by the spring of 1843, when Henry was only six months old, he suffered a severe nervous breakdown. For no reason that he could explain, he was suddenly overwhelmed by a "day-nightmare," a spectral vision that filled him with abject terror and reduced him to a "helpless infancy." Consulting a Dr. J. J. Garth Wilkinson, he was told that what he had experienced was a "vastation," an annihilating of selfhood preceding the influx of new spiritual life. James, Sr., and Dr. Wilkinson, a disciple of the religious mystic Emmanuel Swedenborg, entered into a long and close friendship, and James, Sr., too, became deeply affected by Swedenborg, who provided the basis for all of his subsequent speculations on religion.

After this conversion and period abroad, the Jameses returned to America, where the three younger James children were born—Garth Wilkinson, in 1845; Robertson, in 1846; and Alice, in 1848. For two years (Henry's third and fourth), the family lived in Albany, in a compound of other Jameses and in a house near that of James, Sr.'s widowed mother; but by 1847 they returned again to New York City, settling into a new house on West Fourteenth Street, near Sixth Avenue. Henry's early impressions of New York during this period have been recorded by him elaborately in his autobiographical *A Small Boy and Others*.[3] It was a world that involved him precociously in childhood reading and theater-going; a domestic scene in which James, Sr., was a foremost figure who retired mysteriously into his study, lined with the red-backed volumes of his vast collection of Swedenborg's writings, to work at formulating his "ideas"; a house visited by writers and artists, and by an array of reformers like Parke Godwin and George Ripley, many of them associated with the Brook Farm socialist commune. James, Sr.'s "ideas," however, also extended to education, and for this reason he "gravely pondered," as he expressed it to Emerson, "whether it would not be better to go abroad for a few years with [the children], allowing them to absorb French and German and get a better sensuous education than they are likely to get here."[4] In June, 1855, when Henry was twelve, the Jameses left for Europe.

Abroad, the children were sometimes educated privately, and at other times sent to a variety of different schools, since James, Sr., could not decide which system of education would suit them best. The Jameses, furthermore, moved from country to country, from place to place. They resided for a time in Geneva, then in Paris and London, only to return to France, to live at Boulogne-sur-Mer. After several years, they returned to America, settling at

Newport; then once again they removed to Europe, spending a year in Switzerland and Germany. This experience proved bewildering to the young Jameses, and William would later say of it that the father had given them no real education at all. To Henry, however, their migrations seemed very much an "education," giving him his first, if still limited, access to the romantic "otherness" of Europe that would furnish his imaginative life.

In the autumn of 1860, the Jameses returned to Newport, where they remained until the spring of 1862. There young James lived in an environment unlike that of the rest of the country, preoccupied by business or commercial interests. Both James and his closest friend of this time, Thomas Sergeant Perry, were immersed in literature, particularly the literature of Europe. Europe was present in many ways. William was then studying art under William Morris Hunt, who had lived and worked abroad, and had brought Paris with him to Newport. Another member of James's circle was John LaFarge, who had spent his youth in Paris, where, at his parents' home, he had glimpsed Sainte-Beuve, Baudelaire, Flaubert, and the Goncourts. He lent James his copies of the *Revue des Deux Mondes*, and encouraged his reading of French writers, particularly Balzac, George Sand, Musset, and Mérimée.

In April, 1861, as William and Henry began to face the problem of a vocation, the Civil War erupted. Neither enlisted for duty in the Union Army and much later in life, in *Notes of a Son and Brother*,[5] Henry would write a curious account of an "obscure hurt," suffered while attempting to put out a stable fire, at the "same dark hour" as the onset of the war—an attempt, perhaps, to explain his failure to take part. Leon Edel, the most comprehensive of his biographers, has shown, however, that James's injury did not occur with the outbreak of the war, but a full six months later. The injury itself, wrapped in mystification by James's prose (it was both "extraordinarily intimate" yet "awkwardly irrelevant"), seems to have been a sacroiliac strain, which affected him painfully at different times in his life but was not gravely disabling. Yet, in a sense, the onset of the war did result in a wound, for it forced James to confront his ineffectuality in the active world of men. In the same year as his "psychic wound," his younger brothers enlisted in the Union Army, and went on to distinguish themselves in combat. The more brilliant older sons, William and Henry, "sat out" the war.

In the autumn of 1861, William abandoned art to study chemistry at the Lawrence Scientific School at Harvard; and a year later Henry enrolled in the Harvard Law School. An odd year in residence for him it must have been, since there is no indication that he ever read law, devoting himself instead wholly to literature. By the end of 1864 he made his first, tentative appearances in print, with an unsigned story in the *Atlantic*, and a first review in the *North American Review*. A year later his first signed story was published, and he began to contribute reviews to the *Nation*, newly founded by E. L. Godkin. His early efforts also brought him into contact with a number of editors with whom he would later be on familiar terms. James Russell Lowell and Charles Eliot Norton then jointly edited the *North American Review*, and he would know them both abroad, and with Norton, an art scholar and lover of Italy, and his sister Grace, would carry on a correspondence for many years. Important also was his meeting with W. D. Howells, who arrived in Cambridge in 1866, to become assistant editor of the *Atlantic*, and would publish some of James's best-known novels serially in the magazine.

During this Cambridge period, in 1864, the James parents moved to Boston to be near their sons, and in 1866 to Cambridge itself, settling into a house that faced Harvard Yard, at 20 Quincy Street. Both William and Henry lived at the family home during the middle and late 1860s, as they struggled to establish themselves. Establishing themselves, achieving financial and personal independence, would be a long and arduous process. The stresses James felt at this time are suggested by the family house itself, a house of some ambivalence. E. L. Godkin describes a visit to the Jameses in which a free-for-all discussion takes place that is as lively and witty as any he has ever witnessed, and he gives an impression of a house of high spirits. Yet Lilla Cabot (who married James's friend T. S. Perry) has described a "stiff," oppressive house; and in letters of this time James seems to bear out her impression. In a letter of 1867, he describes the house as being "about as lively as the inner sepulchre."[6] Confined to Quincy Street, while he yearned for "life," clearly involved frustration. Indeed, the house was the setting of marked inner tensions, and of nervous breakdown. William suffered such a breakdown in his earlier years, and was afflicted with an array of illnesses of an apparently psychoneurotic nature that disabled him at times so that he was unable to work. His whole career can be viewed as a struggle to overcome such invalidism through enormous effort of will; and in Henry's case, a threatened or real helplessness is countered by an imperious will toward masterful assertion.

The impression of a "family syndrome" is strengthened by the nervous invalidism of their sister Alice,[7] whose life has at last been presented in detail in Jean Strouse's recent biography *Alice James*. Wracked by an inner intensity that she shared with her older brothers, but denied the outlet of their intellectual or creative expression, she was subject to nervous breakdowns in her teenaged years and throughout her life. Her nerves were so highly strung that if conversations became too exciting she fainted, and she spent periods of time under the care of physicians. Her prostrations suggest both thwarted self-assertion and a marked degree of sexual repression in the James family. It might be noted that although the most outgoing of the younger Jameses, William did not experience his first love affair until he was thirty-four years of age; and that, in *The Principles of Psychology*, he assigns the sexual impulse, as opposed to culturally purposive activity, to the lower compartments of the human brain.[8] In the case of Henry, no love affairs or sexual indulgences of any kind have ever come to light. Favored over the other children by a doting mother, and known within the family as "Angel," he would relate to women guardedly, and always, so far as is known, on a Platonic basis. James's sexual repressions, bred in a Victorian world and a remarkable house, have a bearing on his fiction—its sometimes chilled recoil from sexuality that recalls the Puritans, its elaborate sexual-psychological indirection.

It would be misleading, however, to imply that the legacy of the James family consisted largely of strenuous debilities heroically overcome. The parents lavished their love on their children, and James, Sr., made practically a career of raising them. He gave them a strong sense of family identity, and a set of standards by which to measure themselves and the world. Within the family, Henry found his earliest audience for his pursuit of excellence in literature, as well as generous support and encouragement. His letters to them from abroad show the high level of culture that existed within the family;[9] and, in a way, James's will to triumph in art was also a will to vindicate the Jameses. As an adult living in Europe he would still write that nothing "gives me so much pleasure ... as the feeling of being 'acceptable' " to the members of the James household.[10] Even very late in his life, after a long residence in England, the same note is struck. Summing up his impression of Henry in a letter to his wife, William would write that, despite his foreign excrescences, he "is really ... a native of the James family, and has no other country."[11]

James, Sr., the influential patriarch of the family, is sometimes described as a "mystical democrat," a phrase that perhaps needs clarification. He emerged in a time of intense religious seeking in America, and participated, particularly, in the line of inquiry growing out of what William Ellery Channing called "the moral argument against Calvinism." In the course of his life, he published more than a dozen books—including *Christianity the Logic of Creation* (1857), *The Secret of Swedenborg* (1869), and *Society the Redeemed Form of Man* (1879). All dealt with, without resolving, the same questions. Most fundamentally, James, Sr., repudiated Calvinism's harsh and inscrutable judgments upon mankind. True religion or spirituality, to James, Sr., did not exist on a level above or apart from man, but within his own nature. He retained from Calvinism the conception of a Fall and a Redemption, but worked out the concept in different terms. For him, man's original sin consisted of self-centered being, or *proprium*, from which flow all the world's evils. And he looks to a "transformation-scene," in which the individual will shed his pride in self to find a new sense of self in the divinity within man's nature. Democracy is important in this apocalyptic vision because it brings the "transformation-scene" to the point of imminence. Not in Europe or England, encrusted with ancient institutions that foster a narrow sense of self, and keep men apart, but in America, in the democracy of which the self finds a redemption and completion in a divine sociality with the selfhood of others, will this come about.

This would not be the place to enter into a discussion of James, Sr., and his thinking. But it might be noted briefly that he is very distinctly part of Henry's "cultural" background. In their attitudes toward democracy, the father and son could hardly be further apart, but in other ways the father was influential. He was, for one thing, a gifted writer, with a robust sense of humor, a carica-turist of those he met. A strain of the most irreverent humor con-stantly breaks out in his expression, and perhaps no one has written with more piquant satire of New Englanders—with the exception of his son. The flashing, sardonic humor of James, Sr., seems to have been transmitted to William and Henry, and indeed to Alice, for all of them possess it. In the upbringing he gave his children, he discouraged whatever might narrow their attitudes or their sense of personal identity. His travels back and forth between America and Europe were designed to give them a chance to experience different points of view, before judging on too narrow a basis—to "form" themselves instead of being formed by their environment. His lack of affiliation with groups and organizations, his individual-istic philosophy, and absorption with the individual's inner ex-perience, all eventually affected Henry's attitudes. Through his father first, and then through his Calvinist background, James comes distinctly out of a Protestant tradition.

Chapter Two
Watch and Ward :
A Parable
of Love and Art

Background

Genesis and Text.   In February, 1869, during the period that leads up to *Watch and Ward*,[1] James crossed the Atlantic to begin his eventful "Grand Tour" of Europe. His earlier exposure to the Continent had been in his adolescence; but now, as he approached his twenty-sixth year, he confronted Europe as an adult, as a young man whose career as a writer had already begun. The sense of a new liberation and self-enlargement fills his letters of this time, making it clear how much this first adult experience of Europe meant to him.

After settling in London, James traveled in the countryside, and visited England's great landmarks. From Oxford, he wrote to his brother William: "As I stood last evening within the precincts of mighty Magdalen, gazed at its great serene tower and uncapped my throbbing brow in the wild dimness of its courts, I thought that the heart of me would crack with the fulness of satisfied desire. It is, as I say, satisfied desire that you feel here. . . . The whole place gives me a deeper sense of English life than anything yet."[2]

9

Only two years later, Clement Searle in "A Passionate Pilgrim" will feel similar emotions at Oxford, but they will be made ironic by James's greater detachment and larger perspective than his.

In May, he crossed the Channel to Europe, traveling to Switzerland, and then journeying, for the first time, to Italy. Determined to miss nothing, he made the trip partly by foot, hiking through the Alpine country of the St. Gothard pass, before reaching Milan. By September, passing through a series of famous Italian towns, he arrived in Venice; and by October, after Venice and Florence, he came to Rome, the color and pageantry of which made the most powerful impression upon him of all. "I went reeling and moaning thro' the streets," he wrote to William, "in a fever of enjoyment."[3] In the spring of 1870, after fifteen spirited months abroad, he returned to his family's home in Cambridge, to resume a life that, by comparison with all that he had seen, seemed meager indeed.

His experience abroad, however, enriched the fiction he wrote in Cambridge almost immediately. "A Passionate Pilgrim" (1871), inspired by his impressions of England, was his first major short story, his first use of the international theme that he would elaborate throughout his career. He was also encouraged to attempt his first novel, *Watch and Ward*. By the end of the summer of 1870, he submitted three parts of the five-part work to James T. Fields, editor of the *Atlantic*, where it was serialized from August to December, 1871. James's letter to Fields, accompanying the manuscript, suggests that he had at first held great hopes for the work; but by the time the serialization began in the *Atlantic*, he wrote of it to Norton in very modest terms. "The subject," he remarked, "is something slight; but I have tried to make a work of art.... A certain form will be its chief merit."[4] *Watch and Ward* was not published in book form until 1878, after it was revised by James for style.[5] The critical reception of the novel was generally unfavorable,[6] and it has been regarded since that time as a very slight work, even as a curiosity of James's apprenticeship. *Watch and Ward* was not published in England during James's lifetime, nor was it included by him in the New York

Edition. Its chief interest today is in what it reveals of James at the beginning of his career as a novelist.

   Source and Influence. The plot of *Watch and Ward* is bizarre. Roger Lawrence, a diffident, nearsighted man of twenty-eight, encounters and adopts a twelve-year-old orphan, Nora Lambert, and raises her with the hope of making her his future, ideal wife. Strangely, James does not treat this abnormal situation, which might, as one critic has remarked, "have originated in Hawthorne's notebook . . . or in Freud's,"[7] as being in any way immoral or neurotic. His conception is so peculiar that it would seem difficult to account for. There are, it is true, scores of young girls who become wards in English Gothic novels. *Uncle Silas* (1864), by the Irish novelist Joseph Sheridan LeFanu, comes out of this tradition, in its depiction of Maud Ruthyn, a girl of twelve at the beginning of the novel, who is taken to live with her uncle at his isolated and eerie Bartram-Hough country house, where she is subjected to psychological terror. But this romance of terror is exactly what *Watch and Ward* is not.

   A number of possible sources for *Watch and Ward* have been suggested, but one seems to me convincing—Oliver Wendell Holmes's novel *The Guardian Angel* (1867).[8] At the time James's novel was written Holmes enjoyed a great reputation; his novels were popular in America in the period just after the Civil War; and his associations with the *Atlantic*, for which *Watch and Ward* was written, were extremely close. Holmes had helped to launch the magazine in 1857, and was its most welcome contributor, as well as an editorial advisor; and it may have occurred to James, in writing his apprenticeship novel, that the *Atlantic* would be receptive to a work somewhat in the mode of Holmes's popular one.

   The American setting of *Watch and Ward*, and the situation it treats of an orphaned girl who must choose in marriage among several men, only one of whom is worthy of her, has essential similarities with *The Guardian Angel*. The heroine of *The Guardian Angel* is named Myrtle Hazard, and as her last name implies, some risk accompanies her appraisal of the men who, for various reasons, are drawn to her. One is a clergyman, the Reverend Joseph Stoker, whom she has idealized, only to find that while talking of heaven he has been more interested in the attractiveness of young girls. Another is an ambitious lawyer, Murray Bradshaw, cast in the role of villain. The worldly cleric and the lawyer ambitious to rise in the world are characters Myrtle must gauge correctly before her future happiness can be realized. These characters have counterparts in James's Hubert Lawrence and George Fenton in *Watch and Ward*; and their likeness draws attention to other similarities.

Like James's Nora Lambert, Myrtle Hazard is an orphan who blooms into a beautiful young woman by the end of the work. The local schoolmaster, Byles Gridley, sends her to a fashionable school, at a distance from the village of Oxbow, and when she returns, at seventeen, she has not only been improved by her association with society and culture, but has also become astonishingly beautiful. Such a pattern is seen in *Watch and Ward*, with the difference that the more cosmopolitan James sends Nora off for a year in Italy for her transforming experience. It should also be noted that the hero of *The Guardian Angel*, Clement Lindsay, is an artist. When Myrtle is fifteen and he is twenty, he rescues her from drowning, and then creates a statue bust so much inspired by her as to take possession of his mind. "It was too nearly," Holmes writes, "like the story of the ancient sculptor; his own work was an overmatch for its artist." Holmes obviously refers here to Pygmalion, who, in Greek myth, creates a statue of a young woman, only to become enamoured of her beauty; and after the gods have endowed her with life, in answer to his prayers, he marries her, weds his own ideal. At the end of *The Guardian Angel*, Clement Lindsay marries Myrtle Hazard—not, however, by deception, fraud, or attempted coercion practiced by other characters in the novel, but by allowing her to choose freely. He has never told her, even, that it was he who had rescued her from drowning two years earlier, for he has not wished to force a claim on her gratitude. "I wanted," he explains at the end, "a free gift."

Clement Lindsay and James's Roger Lawrence do not seem very

similar; yet there is a marked likeness in the roles they play. As the guardian and sponsor of Nora, Roger has an artistlike function. He "creates" Nora from crude materials and endows her with life. The Pygmalion myth implied in Holmes's conception of Clement Lindsay and Myrtle Hazard can also be noticed in James's conception of Roger Lawrence and Nora Lambert. In both cases, the "artist"-lovers respect the "freedom" of their creations. Roger, sounding very much like Clement, remarks: "I wish to leave her free and take the risk" (108).[9] And the endings of the novels are similar. Confronting the risks of choice, discovering for themselves the difference between appearance and reality, the heroines finally and "freely" choose the heroes, and there are happy endings. A complication exists in Roger Lawrence, however, since he derives not only from Clement but also from another male character in Holmes's novel, Byles Gridley, the schoolmaster. Gridley has the role of Myrtle's disinterested benefactor and guardian (even "guardian angel"); it is he who provides her with opportunities for transformation, during her period away from Oxbow, and shields her from folly and error. Clement Lindsay is her lover who does not speak—until the end—but is her rightful mate, since he alone, among those who are attracted to her, respects her inner nature. In *Watch and Ward*, in a daring stroke, guardian and lover become one in the person of Roger Lawrence.

The Problem of Form

Although a serious work, *Watch and Ward* is not devoid of humor or satire, as certain of the characters reveal. A character rich in comic possibilities is Mrs. Keith, who twice rejects Roger's proposal of marriage, before becoming his confidante and matchmaker. At the end one sees her opening and shutting her fan, as she claims credit before a social group for Roger's marriage to Nora, and one smiles, not only because her gesture reveals that she sees the marriage in terms of personal vanity, but also because, given one's previous knowledge of her, it is exactly the type of remark she *would* make. Mrs. Keith belongs very much to the world of courtship; it is her peculiar ambiance, and defines the limits of her personal existence. On her first appearance, she is fully revealed in her ambitions through matrimony; and when she returns to Boston later, following her marriage abroad to a remarkably short-lived husband, she is what she was always intended to be by nature—a comfortably settled widow, "with diamonds in her dressing-case and her carriage in her stable" (110). Pert and coquettish, she has intelligence of a specialized and limited kind rather than moral understanding. It is characteristic of her that she should favor Roger's courtship of Nora only after she has examined his bank balance. It is characteristic, too, that she should rout the interloper Hubert Lawrence with sallies of wit and double entendre. "I have done him an injustice," she remarks archly, as Hubert retreats from her drawing room, "I fancied him light, but I see he's vicious" (169).

Mrs. Keith, however, suggests a work of a different kind than *Watch and Ward* actually is. James's satire depends upon nuance, requiring complex social situations that are not found in the novel. What it presents, instead, are characters conceived as types, and situations conditioned by melodrama. The suicide of Mr. Lambert, Nora's woe-begone and debt-ridden father, belongs to the conventions of the Victorian stage. Beside his dead body, James writes, "stood a little girl in her nightdress, her long hair on her shoulders, shrieking and wringing her hands... 'O father, father, father!' sobbed the little girl" (29). Hubert Lawrence is depicted at the beginning as a clergyman with an unsteady moral sense, and his behavior thereafter is predictable. He takes advantage of Roger's illness to ingratiate himself with Nora, even though he is already engaged to a young woman in New York; and in a final scene his superficiality becomes obvious even to Nora. James not only exposes Hubert in this scene, he also humiliates him. Breaking down, and passing his hands woefully over his face, he cries, "Say it outright, [Nora]; you despise me!" (231).

George Fenton, another claimant to Nora, is patently a villain; he is revealed as villainish on his first appearance, a man, as James writes, "incapable of any other relation to a fact than a desire to turn it to pecuniary account" (80). Moreover, with his tattooed hand, diamond tie pin, and coarse dealings in the West, he is less an individual than a specimen of a social class. Always on the scent of money, he looks up his distant cousin Nora, hoping to profit by her association with Roger. His professed fondness for Nora is contradicted by the revelation of his inner thoughts as to how he may make use of her; and in New York, when she comes to him in her confusion, he attempts to blackmail Roger with the threat of darkening Nora's reputation. He even holds her under duress in a house in the city, under the eye of his friend Mrs. Paul. In the end, however, Nora faces him down, and makes her way past him to the door, while he sinks into a chair, buries his face in his hands, and cries, "O Lord! I am an ass!" (227). His last appearance in the novel, like Hubert's, has the form of a humiliation scene.

In a novel as melodramatically plotted as *Watch and Ward*, satire has no room to expand; the detached, observing intelligence upon which satire thrives is continually checked by the banalities of situation. Plot, indeed, comes to have a dominance over characterization. In a notable essay on *Watch and Ward*, J. A. Ward has commented on the subservience of character to plot, and noted its effect on James's conception of Roger Lawrence, who is essentially cut off from the other characters. "The major device," Ward writes,

is the happy ending. Another is the use of the secondary characters as obstacles to the happiness of the hero and heroine; these minor characters are made into a gallery of knowing and unknowing villains whose only function is to impede the success of Roger's plan.... Rather soon after *Watch and Ward*, James would use secondary characters not so much to block or further the action, but to form "rela tions" with the protagonist ... these relations contribute to the revelation of the secondary character's identity and also become the materials that are seized upon and tirelessly interpreted by this character's intelligence. There is little suggestion in *Watch and Ward* that the secondary characters reveal anything important about Roger or even stimulate his intelligence. Roger, a rarity among James's protagonists, really possesses an autonomous existence; he is detachable from the characters who surround him.[10]

Ward considers *Watch and Ward*, however, in terms of its surface realism, giving only slight attention to another mode of imagination in the work, that of romance.

The Use of Romance

On the surface, *Watch and Ward* is an unconventional story using the most conventional character types and plot devices of Victorian fiction. Yet beneath this surface, it is pure romance, involving the reader in an atmosphere of wonder that cannot be apprehended by reason merely, and is expressed frequently through fairy tale and myth. At one point, James refers to Nora, in her torn frock and orphaned state, as being "like a beggar maid in a ballad" (231), an allusion to the English ballad "King Cophetua and the Beggar Maid," later the subject of Tennyson's famous poem "The Beggar Maid." The final lines of Tennyson's poem foretell the marvel of Nora's destiny: "Cophetua sware a royal oath; / 'This beggar maid shall be my queen!' " In James's romance treatment, the reader responds to Nora not only as a "beggar maid" but also as spiritual royalty.

As a beggar maid transformed, Nora is also a version of Cinderella. Like Cinderella, she is given a fairy godmother, and attends a great ball, at which she herself becomes resplendent; achieves, in other words, her true or inner nature. From Rome, Nora writes to Roger: "I came out six weeks ago at the great ball of the Princess X . . . but Mrs. Keith is a fairy god-mother; she shod me in glass slippers and we went" (132). And not only does she attend the princess's ball, she herself is evoked frequently as a "princess" or a princess *en herbe*, as in the early scene in which she is introduced to Hubert. "She came sidling into the room," James writes, "with a rent in her short-waisted frock, and the *Child's Own Book* in her hand, with her finger in the history of *The Discreet Princess*" (49). On Christmas Eve, Nora thinks of what her life might have been like, a life of "wandering and begging," if Roger had not adopted her. "I feel to-night," she exclaims, thinking of her amazing good fortune as Roger's ward, "like a princess in a fairy tale" (64–65); and the novel's happy ending, the union of prince and princess, on the basis of nobility of worth, belongs to a fairy-tale convention.

Carrying the analogy further, Nora is likened to a particular princess of fairy tale, the Princess Badoura of the *Arabian Nights.* During his convalescence from a serious illness, Roger regains consciousness to become aware, at first unclearly, of the figure of a woman, framed by a window flooded with brilliant sunlight. "She was no vision," James comments,

> . . . this image was fixed and radiant. He half closed his eyes. . . . There came to him out of his boyish past, a vague, delightful echo of the "Arabian Nights." The room was gilded by the autumn sunshine into the semblance of an enamelled harem court; he himself seemed a languid Persian, lounging on musky cushions; the fair woman at the window a Scheherazade, a Badoura. . . . She smiled and smiled, and, after a little, as he only stared confusedly, she blushed, not like Badoura or Scheherazade, but like Nora. (178)

In the *Arabian Nights*, the Princess Badoura and the Prince Camaralzaman are lovers, each the ideal of the other, who belong to geographically distant worlds yet manage miraculously to meet. At one point in the tale, the princess is awakened and restored from an illness by the prince; and this idea is insinuated, although sexual roles are reversed, in the scene in which Roger is restored to life by his "recovery" of Nora, the ideal that sustains him. His recovery belongs as much to the world of romance as Nora's miraculous transformation abroad.

The romance quality of the work is reinforced by James's use of myth. At the beginning, referring to his early infatuation with Mrs. Keith, Roger reflects that he "had made a woman a goddess, and she had made him a fool" (29). Mrs. Keith is no goddess, but Nora is compared to one. Midway in the work, comparing Nora with other young women, some making a stronger first impression, Roger reflects that Nora, nevertheless, "revealed that deep-

shrined natural force, lurking in the shadow of modesty like a
statue in a recess, which you hardly know whether to denominate
humility or pride" (124). The shrined statue in a recess links
Nora with Athena, an association implied again in the passage
where Nora appears in Roger's sick room, framed by a window
with a statuesque effect, like an "image radiant and fixed" (178).
The association is fully specified when Nora returns from Europe.
"A singular harmony and serenity," James remarks,

> seemed to pervade her person. Her beauty lay in no inordinate per-
> fection of the individual features, but in deep sweet fellowship that
> reigned between smile and step and glance and tone. The total effect
> was an impression of the simplest and yet the richest loveliness. "Pallas
> Athene," said Hubert to himself, "sprang fully-armed, we are told,
> from the brain of Jove. But we have a Western version of the myth.
> She was born in Missouri." (145)

These allusions are reminders of alternative values at issue in the
work, the difference between the subordinate characters and Roger
and Nora, who have strength in modesty, and are affiliated with
the more evolved "wisdom" of Athena.

Through such analogies of fairy tale and myth, James implies
the mystery of inwardness and the potentialities of being that are
continually at odds with the subordinate characters' severely restricted natures. Mrs. Keith is defined as rigidly as she can be by
her allegiance to fact, to dollars and cents, but she is eclipsed by
Nora, who has the capacity for wondrous growth. James refers,
in connection with Nora, to *ewig Weibliche*, the "eternal feminine"—the principle of inwardness, fecundity, and endless evolution; and Nora has a romantic heightening through this association.
The apparent oddity in the novel that a number of the women
have last names that are the first names of men—Miss Morton, who
later becomes Mrs. Keith, and Fenton's friend Mrs. Paul—is explained when one sees that through this device James has contrasted
them negatively to Nora, who alone has the potentialities for
growth and development of the "eternal feminine."

The marvel of Nora's growth into beauty, and finally "wisdom," is dramatized by an elaborate play of imagery, linking her with the natural world. Sunlight, the color blue (for the sky or heavens), flowers and blooms, form imagistic patterns that accrue through the novel. Nora is sometimes shown against a sunlit background, or is framed by brilliant sunlight, and in Italy she blooms into ripeness "in the sunshine of a great contentment" (145). Early in the work, Roger observes young Nora patiently, "as a wandering botanist [looks] for the first woodland violets, ... for the shy field-flower of spontaneous affection" (46); and in regard to Nora, Fenton would like to "pluck the rose from so thornless a tree" (82). Women, to him, are "mostly as cut flowers, blooming awhile in the waters of occasion, but yielding no second or rarer satisfaction" (82). These cut flowers, arranged in a vase for a time, have a wholly different implication than the blooms associated with Nora, which have the suggestion of the living power of nature. During Roger's convalescence, "the flower of [Nora's] beauty had bloomed in a night, that of his passion in a day" (179), metaphors that form a contrast to Fenton's artificiality. All of these images come together in the climactic scene, when Nora leaves Hubert's apartment to find Roger approaching in the street, the point at which their love blooms into being. "The sky," James comments, "was blazing blue overhead; the opposite side of the street was all in sun" (236).

But what *Watch and Ward* also reveals at the end is that James's realism and romance in the work fail to fuse. One can believe James's romance evocation of Nora much more than his conception of her in terms of realism. The difficulties Nora encounters are patently contrived, and cannot provide a believable basis for the recognition of love for Roger that is imputed to her. The ending shows, particularly, the clash between the "organic form" of romanticism (implied in the novel's natural imagery) and the artificiality of James's plot. James's use of romance is, in fact, strikingly more sophisticated and effective than his handling of surface realism. In this disparity of form, the novel offers a vantage point from which to observe James's development, for in his next novel, *Roderick Hudson*, a fusion of realism and romance is fully and successfully achieved.

The Inner Story

James's playing off of a surface realism with romance creates for the reader a sense of living in different worlds at once—one time-bound, the other timeless; one severely "fixed," the other "free"; one belonging to fact, the other to imagination. And this duality in the work calls attention to an additional feature of the novel, its parabolic "inner story." Central to the inner story is Roger Lawrence, whose appearance is foreshadowed in certain of the early stories leading up to *Watch and Ward*. The fear of sex, or more specifically the threat of a woman's sexuality, enters into a number of these stories, but in two—"The Story of a Year" (1865) and "A Most Extraordinary Case" (1868)—distinctively. One is set at the beginning and the other at the end of the Civil War, and their heroes are wounded veterans who return to confront their incapacity for physical love and romance. Their role as veterans, however, is not at all convincing. The war is remote in the stories even as background, and nothing about the heroes suggests that they have been familiar with bivouacs or battles. They are most credible as civilians, men of inwardness and highly subjective consciousness—artists, in fact, of the type of James himself.

At the opening of "The Story of a Year," John Ford takes a sunset walk with his fiancée as he is about to leave for service in the war, and as he does so he points to the fiery sun sinking below the horizon, and remarks that its extinction "is an allegory." More nearly, the story itself is an allegory, for at the end Ford dies, not from his supposed wounds but from a recognition—that he is unfit for the active world. Dying, he resembles a Greek whose glance lingers over the sculptured Artemis, who is both a symbol of chastity and an embodied work of art. "A Most Extraordinary Case" is an enlargement of the story and its allegory. The invalid veteran Ferdinand Mason, a man of "habitual reserve" who has read a

library of books, dies when he falls in love, or is confronted with
the reality of physical love. Able to meditate upon no "other
mistress" than "work, letters, philosophy, fame," said, too, to be
the most "promising" young man of his generation in America,
he strongly suggests James himself. Neither Ford nor Mason, as
characters with artist identities that are somewhat thinly concealed,
is able to come to any kind of terms with life; all that they can
do is to retreat into death. But in *Watch and Ward*, a new version
of the type appears, an artist surrogate who not only survives his
encounter with the world, but is actually allowed to succeed in it
very much on his own terms.

It is true, on the surface at least, that Roger Lawrence, with his
meek habits and apparent lack of a vocation, has little resemblance
to an artist. But the idea of the artist is seen in his adoption and
guidance of Nora toward his ideal. He "creates" Nora from shabby
circumstances and unpromising materials, and fashions her into
his conception. The myth of Pygmalion, who falls in love with
and weds his own conception, is implied throughout *Watch and
Ward*, and this analogy also makes Roger a "sculptor" of a kind.
James's allusions to Athena reinforce the art association, too, for
Athena was the goddess-protectress of art, of the mind and hand,
of craftsmanship and self-realization. She represents the striving for
a higher justice or wisdom through aspiration and discipline, and
is Roger's ideal, as the imagery of the novel bears out. In Italy,
Nora acquires a fullness of beauty having the attributes of Athena—
harmony, grace, and proportion, the "form" of the Jamesian artist.

A theme word used to characterize Roger at the end is "integrity," and his integrity is seen in his devotion to an ideal. His
ideal of Nora may appear Quixotic, even laughable to certain of
the other characters; Roger is disarmingly modest and seemingly
unassertive, and the chances against his success are enormous. Yet
by the end he does succeed, and the reader is forced to revise his
estimate of Roger, whose patience and discipline have been acts
of faith. In the same year that James wrote *Watch and Ward*, he
achieved his first masterpiece in the short story form, "A Passionate
Pilgrim," which depicts an American's awakening to art, beauty,

and love in England. In a sense, Roger Lawrence is a passionate pilgrim in America; and at times his preparing himself to be worthy of the Nora-who-is-to-be is even described in terms of a holy pilgrimage. He studies a library of books, and travels across the globe in order to know the world; he trains himself for his role as assiduously as an earnest aspirant to art. "He travelled," James remarks, "in a spirit of solemn attention, like some grim devotee of a former age making a pilgrimage for the welfare of the one he loved" (54).

During the course of his pilgrimage, Roger is at times faced with setbacks, and is even tempted to lose faith. When Nora returns from Italy transformed, he suffers an illness during which he loses confidence in his ability to see his plan through. But when he regains consciousness, his vision of Nora as a steady and fixed ideal restores him to health. The physician who attends him remarks: "It was a Daniel come to judgment. . . . I verily believe she saved him" (172). This allusion to Daniel underscores the theme of faith, since it is absolute fidelity to God that Daniel represents in the Old Testament; a faith, no matter what outward circumstances might seem to indicate, in God's ultimate justice and vindication, in a glorious reward for the faithful. In his fidelity to his imaginative commitment, Roger earns his association with the artist of integrity.

Roger is tested, as a matter of fact, more than once. In the symmetrical arrangement of characters James has already begun to employ, Nora is tempted by two men (Hubert and Fenton) while Roger is tempted by two women (Teresita in Lima and Miss Sands in New York). But Roger is also tempted to compromise his ideals by making sexual "use" of Nora, taking advantage of his position and her innocence. Two passages in *Watch and Ward* that are charged with sexual innuendo are notable. One occurs when Fenton stays with Roger and Nora, and Roger wonders if Fenton's attentions to Nora might not serve to clear the way for him with the girl. "The ground," James remarks, "might be gently tickled to receive his own sowing; the petals of the young girl's nature, playfully forced apart, would leave the golden heart of the flower but the more accessible to his own vertical rays" (81). The sexual imagery of this passage is startling.

Startling, too, is the imagery of a somewhat later passage. While Hubert is visiting Roger, Nora enters the room at bedtime, and asks for Roger's key with which to wind her watch. "Roger's key," James comments, "proved a complete misfit, so that she had recourse to Hubert's. It hung on the watch-chain which depended on his waistcoat, and some rather intimate fumbling was needed to adjust it to Nora's diminutive timepiece. It worked admirably" (109). Leon Edel has written that the sexual imagery of this passage was naively unconscious on James's part, yet it is suggestive to an extraordinary degree. Hubert asks Roger if there is not a "danger" in his relationship to Nora. *Is* she only a child? he asks. It is at this moment that Nora appears, dressed for bed in a blue merino robe, her long amber hair "unloosed" from its coil. The whole passage is intended to be erotic, to show the temptation Roger might have yielded to but does not.

In his fidelity and self-denial, Roger is contrasted to Hubert and Fenton. Roger and Hubert are clearly intended to be compared, as cousins and characters possessing the same last name. Both have "divine" missions, Roger his devotion to his ideal of Nora, Hubert his pastorate. But if Hubert has a spiritual calling, he is unlike Roger in his lack of faith. His sophistry is apparent when he tells Nora that "if my love wrestles with my faith, as the angel with Jacob, and if my love stands uppermost, I will admit it's a fair game. Faith is faith under a hundred forms" (163). Hubert, furthermore, is linked with Fenton, whose life is a repudiation of high ideals. "The Knight of La Mancha," James writes, describing Fenton, "never urged his quaint steed with a grimer pressure of the knees than that with which Fenton held himself erect on the hungry hobby of success" (81). Hubert and Fenton are similar, too, in their relation to Nora, for both regard her selfishly, Hubert for his own pleasure, Fenton for material gain. Both are specifically called "egotists," and, having strictly worldly values, they are incapable of any transcendence of self.

When, at the end, Roger declares, "My dear Nora, what have

we to do with Hubert's young girls" (238), he announces their affiliation with spirit as against world. The same is implied in this passage when James says of Nora that "she was in the secret of the universe, and the secret of the universe was, that Roger was the only man in it who had a heart" (236). Roger's having a "heart" suggests much more than that he possesses kindness and generosity; it implies that he has a "believing" heart, a spirit and soul. His "heart" is in contrast to the "head" of Hubert and Fenton. who possess intelligence of a kind, but have no educated conscience or moral sense. The contrast between the worldly and the innocent in certain of James's early stories recurs in *Watch and Ward*, in which, in a fairy-tale way, the believers in spiritual reality are rewarded. The worldly characters, on the other hand, those who seemingly possess power, turn out to be powerless. Hubert and Fenton are captured in their frustration and failure in exactly the same way, as they sink into chairs, bury their faces in their hands, and confront their inner emptiness.

As an artist surrogate, Roger also comments on the American setting of *Watch and Ward*. Boston and New York are filled in so lightly as background that they seem hardly to have a distinct identity. Judging from what little is indicated, however, they have very little affinity with spiritual reality. New York, in particular, is seedy both in its physical appearance and in its commercial spirit. When Nora comes to New York near the end, alone and with little money, she enters an establishment identified by a fly-blown sign as a "Ladies' Café," and orders a cup of tea, for which she is charged a dollar. From there she proceeds to the scrap iron business of Franks and Fenton, to discover that Franks has been defrauded by his partner Fenton, magnifying the sense of New York as a scene of vulgar exploitation. Fenton himself has been rather conspicuously cast as a Westerner, but he seems at home in New York even though he does not thrive there, since its money idiom is his own. By making Fenton a Westerner, however, James enlarges the geography of the novel, making the reader feel that it deals with America itself. Its metaphor is scrap iron, coin, and the unexpanded heart. Yet surprisingly enough, James intimates in *Watch and Ward* that the artist may yet succeed with American materials. Nora is also from the West, from St. Louis, and she is said to be a "Western version" of ancient myth in her expansive possibilities of being—guided by Roger's brain and hand. Nothing could be farther from the recoil and failure of the surrogate artists Ford and Mason than Roger's assumption of confidence. Not even the transformation of Nora equals in breadth the transformation in James.

Watch and Ward as a Prediction of the Later Novels

Watch and Ward is usually regarded as an artless work, and thus an anomaly of James's early apprenticeship. But if its romance dimension and inner story are taken into account, it can be seen as being much less artless than has been assumed. It does not, however, succeed as a novel, for its sophisticated inner plot is not matched by a sophisticated outer story. The outer story, with its creaking plot and stereotyped characters, fails to rise above the level of the banal literature it was meant to parody. James fails, too, to make Roger fully credible as the novel's hero, since he remains too locked away within his privacy to be believable when he is supposedly in love with Mrs. Keith, or, later and more seriously, when he woos and wins Nora. The largest interest of the work is still in what it shows of James's future development as a novelist; for it contains many embryonic character types and partially developed themes, all of which are present in the original version of 1871, as an examination of the serial version of the novel confirms.

It is extraordinary how much *Watch and Ward* foreshadows. Mrs. Keith, for example, inaugurates a procession of dowager types who will people James's novels and stories. As friend and matchmaker for Roger, she gives rise to a line of confidantes that range from Mrs. Tristram in *The American* to Maria Gostrey in *The Ambassadors*. A fairy godmother who transports Nora to Europe where she may undergo enlargement, she anticipates Mrs. Touchett in *The Portrait of a Lady*. Roger himself, in his sponsorship of Nora, is an early version of Ralph Touchett. As a Western, stretching his long legs as he sits on a divan, Fenton gives a hint of Christopher Newman; and as an ambitious but unflourishing denizen of New York, he foreshadows Morris Townsend. "At any rate," Fenton reflects, sounding very much like Townsend, "it would do a clever man no harm to have a rich girl foolishly in love with him" (82). And Nora, as the American girl, initiated into experience, and forced to choose among several suitors, will evolve into later heroines, including Isabel Archer herself. She has, furthermore, in her tattered background but romantic growth, affinities with Verena Tarrant in *The Bostonians*.

Significantly, too, James's novelistic concern with art already enters in a number of ways into *Watch and Ward*. When Nora comes upon Hubert near the end, he is posing for an artist whose sketch of him, giving him a spurious ennoblement, reveals his superficiality, his inner emptiness. Miss Sands, perceiving that she cannot be Roger's ideal, is also captured in the imagery of art as she stands for a moment "as motionless as some sculptured statue of renunciation," (219). But James's art metaphor is focused chiefly by Roger Lawrence, his artist surrogate. In his isolation, Roger attempts, as Hawthorne once said, "to open an intercourse with the world." His America, as much as his predecessor's, has material and commercial rather than artistic concerns; but Roger proposes to impose upon it a more "civilized" vision. At the end, winning Nora through virtue, discipline, and self-denial, he does succeed. His success is prophecy, and a strong element of fantasy attaches to it. At its core, *Watch and Ward* is a fantasy prediction of James's success as an artist. It is a prediction, however, that is made problematic by the nature of the hero, who conquers without being able to reach out very far to life, to step outside of his self-enclosure. In later works, James's heroes will be more strenuously tested, and their integrity will be affirmed not so much by their success on the world's terms as by their failure or renunciation.

Chapter Three

Roderick Hudson : Art and Moral Encounter in Rome

Background

Genesis and Text. James remained in Cambridge until May, 1872, when he again embarked for Europe, this time acting as escort to his sister Alice and his aunt Kate. The three journeyed through England, France, and Switzerland during the summer, and in the early autumn through parts of Germany and Italy. After seeing his sister and aunt off to America in October, James then continued on alone in Europe. He spent the remainder of the autumn in Paris, but by December returned to Rome, where he soon became acquainted with its American artist colony, which inspired his conception of the artist colony in *Roderick Hudson*.[1]

A central figure of the American artist colony in Rome was William Wetmore Story, a New Englander who had abandoned the practice of law for the life of a sculptor, and then lived in an opulent style in his forty-room apartment in the Palazzo Barberini. In the same circle was Luther Terry, a painter whose wife was the widow of the American sculptor Thomas Crawford. Others in the group included Harriet Hosmer and Sarah Freeman Clarke, who had mingled with the Transcendentalists; Elizabeth Boott, a painter of modest talents who became a particular friend of James's; and Eugene Benson, a painter of careful but uninspired landscapes. Story was the cynosure of the group and was enjoying a large popularity at the time, but James found his work vastly overvalued; of Story, James wrote to Norton: "I have never seen such a case of *prosperous* pretension."[2] His "detection" of the lesser figures may be imagined, since all of the minor characters in the novel, belonging to the American artist colony, are almost painfully limited in the nature of their gifts.

In late May, 1873, James left Rome for Florence, and there he began work on *Roderick Hudson*, which proved to be a turning point in his career. He was then thirty years old, and although he had published travel sketches, reviews, and stories prolifically, he had not as yet published a novel in book form. At this point, Howells, as editor of the *Atlantic*, entered into a contract with James for the serialization of a Roman novel, which would run for twelve installments, and for which he would be paid $1,000. With work on the novel begun in Florence, and continued for a time in Baden-Baden, James returned to America in the autumn of 1874; and it was in Boston and later in New York that the novel was completed. *Roderick Hudson* began its serialization in the *Atlantic* in January, 1875, the same month *A Passionate Pilgrim*, his first collection of tales, was published. The serialized version was revised by James before it appeared in book form,[3] and was minutely revised twice more—for the first English book edition of 1878, and for the New York Edition, published thirty years later. The revisions do not alter incident or characterization; but for stylistic polish and greater subtlety of shading, the text of the New York Edition is distinctly the preferred version.

Source and Influence.   Although Rowland Mallet, as an initiator of an idealistic project, evolves from Roger Lawrence, his conception was also affected by external sources. James's close, insistent contrasting of Rowland with a more passionate central figure is notably similar to the contrast of temperament employed by Howells in his novel *A Foregone Conclusion* (1875), written just before *Roderick Hudson* and twice reviewed by James, enthusiastically, in the *Nation* and the *North American Review*. *A Foregone Conclusion* deals with Americans in Italy and, like

Roderick Hudson, is a study in thwarted temperament—that of Don Ippolito, the "romantic" character, imprisoned in his old world priesthood in which he no longer believes, and denied the active role and the spacious "freedom" he believes he could find in America; and Ferris, the American consul and "rational" character, who is unable to commit himself, with any force of passion, to life.

Of the novel's characters, Gloriani seems suggested by Story; but the source for Roderick Hudson has been a matter more of speculation than certainty. Several American artists who lived abroad have been suggested as inspirations—William Morris Hunt, and the sculptors Thomas Crawford and Hiram Powers—but none corresponds to Roderick fully. A literary source sometimes noted is *Paul Fane* (1857), a novel by Nathaniel Parker Willis, a friend of James, Sr., that deals with a young man from New England who has an "unconquerable passion" for art, and abandons a safe profession for which he is preparing to become an artist in Rome. But *Paul Fane* has no extended similarities with *Roderick Hudson*, and seems more a precedent than an influence.

Other possible sources include *L'Affaire Clemenceau*, a novel by Alexandre Dumas, *fils*, which James reviewed with enthusiasm eight years before writing *Roderick Hudson*, and which also deals with a sculptor whose involvement in turbulent emotion interferes with his ability to create and leads eventually to his death. Alfred de Musset, to whom James devoted a chapter in *French Poets & Writers*, also seems relevant to Roderick as a "romantic" artist of promise and precocity whose susceptibility to worldly distractions, and particularly women, seriously impaired his faith in his art and his ability to create. Yet no single source accounts entirely for Roderick, who seems modeled largely on a cultural type, that of the romantic artist and doomed "fated" man. German storm and stress poetry, Goethe's *Werther*, and Jean-Jacques Rousseau all furnish an ancestry and predict his emotions.

Many different and rather glancing influences on *Roderick Hudson* derive from James's extensive reading. But these diverse influences are minor compared to the effect on the work of Turgenev and Hawthorne.[4] By 1875, Turgenev had become a discernible influence on James's fiction. It is significant, too, that just before writing *Roderick Hudson*, James read through all of Turgenev's work and published a lengthy essay on him, the most ambitious one he had written on any author up to that time. The essay strongly implies a kinship felt for Turgenev, whom James regarded as the head of the realist school in Europe. One of Turgenev's novels in particular, *Smoke*, has large implications for *Roderick Hudson*, for in it the heroine creates the psychological model for Christina Light. Turgenev's Irina is beautiful, passionate, and willful, a young woman of inner complexity and contradictory desires. She marries General Ratmirov to occupy a place in "society," even though she is contemptuous of its emptiness. She has, as Turgenev remarks, "the morbid melancholy of the lady of fashion who is sick and weary of the world, but cannot live outside its circle." Irina has an actresslike nature, cultivates fictitious emotions in which she convinces herself she believes, and is a snare for men weaker than herself. She is the *femme fatale* who inspires Christina, a *femme fatale* in her every pulsation. Litvinov, the hero of *Smoke*, is "afraid of falling into [Irina's] clutches," but very soon does so; and a markedly similar pattern of susceptibility, inner conflict, and moral failure can be seen in Roderick Hudson in his relationship with Christina.

The antithetical relationships Turgenev works with in *Smoke*, furthermore, are also seen in *Roderick Hudson*. The worldly Irina is contrasted to Turgenev's "pure" girl from the country, Tatyana, Litvinov's fiancée. When Tatyana arrives in Baden-Baden, she finds Litvinóv already under Irina's spell. The young women observe and make judgments of one another, as Christina and Mary Garland, the woman of the world and the girl from the country, do in *Roderick Hudson*. Following this confrontation, Irina persuades Litvinov to break his engagement with Tatyana so that they may, in her inspiration of the moment, go off together. Litvinov breaks his engagement for her sake, but she does not, after all, abandon her place in the fashionable world. For nothing, Litvinov sacrifices his integrity and dishonors his fiancée, a dishonoring of himself and others seen in Roderick. The character contrasts and progression of events in *Smoke* create the pattern for *Roderick Hudson*.

Yet *Roderick Hudson* has a different, more cerebral texture than *Smoke*, and more complicated psychological interests; and it contains no hint of another of James's major characters, Rowland Mallet. Peter Buitenhius has commented persuasively on Hawthorne's Coverdale, the narrator of *The Blithedale Romance*, as Mallet's prototype.[5] Mallet, he points out, has the point-of-view function of Coverdale, whom James, in his biography of Hawthorne, describes as a man whose nature it is to be "half a poet, half a critic, and all a spectator." Both Coverdale and Mallet fall in love with a New England maiden who loves another member of the quartet of characters, and both are left alone at the end with a sense of having failed. Both works are concerned with characters who commit the "unpardonable sin" of violating another's personality. Buitenhuis concludes that "despite all the European influences that were ... working so fruitfully on James's imagination," Hawthorne's character involvements in *The Blithedale Romance* formed the "most powerful determinants" of the subject and technique of *Roderick Hudson*.[6]

The Hawthorne dimension of *Roderick Hudson* is greater even than Buitenhuis suggests, since another of Hawthorne's works, *The Marble Faun*, also enters into James's conception of the novel. *Roderick Hudson* is similar to *The Marble Faun* in its spacious and evocative setting in Rome, and in its treatment of a limited group of characters who belong to its American artist colony. In his handling of this situation, James continually gravitates toward Hawthorne's use of symbolism and allegory. Hawthorne's Rome comes to stand for an ancient European corruption that ultimately implicates American innocence, and the theme of corruption and innocence is central to *Roderick Hudson*. In *The Marble Faun*, works of art have symbolic connotations, implying the characters' inner states and marking out the stages of a fall they enact from innocence into experience; and in *Roderick Hudson*, each of the works of art Roderick creates informs the reader of his inner life, beginning with the bust of a naked youth drinking from a gourd, the figure of innocence about to taste experience, that he creates in Northampton, Massachusetts. Northampton is captured in the imagery of gardens, and gardens—morally indicative ones reminiscent of Hawthorne's—are later used by James to evoke Rome as a sphere of timeless moral encounter.

It is surely no coincidence that soon after arriving in Rome, Roderick should create works representing Adam and Eve, and that, at the end, as he gazes at his statue of the primal Adam, should declare himself "damned." "If I hadn't come to Rome," he cries, "... I shouldn't have fallen" (436).[7] *Roderick Hudson* embraces two traditions at once. It is an achieved novel of manners, minutely precise in its observation of personal relationships; and yet has the symbolic dimension and the large resonance of romance. It is realism and romance fused.

The Diagram of Characters

Although of limited scope, the subordinate characters of *Roderick Hudson* have been solidly created. Mrs. Hudson, with her hair smoothed and confined with "Puritanic precision" (53) and her "meek apprehensive smile" (73), is exactly what she should be. In Rome, she is astray, and out of her element. "When I was a young lady at school," she says, "I remember I had a medal with a pink ribbon for 'proficiency in ancient history'—the seven kings, or is it the seven hills? and Quintus Curtius and Julius Caesar, and—and that period, you know. I believe I have my medal somewhere in a drawer now, but I have forgotten all about the kings" (327). Other characters are struck off with a few, absolutely right strokes. One thinks of Madame Grandoni and her wig, the husband who deserted her for a *prima donna assoluta.* And there is Miss Blanchard, with her prim culture and absence of spontaneity, her pictures of "dew-sprinkled roses, with the dew-drops very highly finished" (10).

Mr. Leavenworth is seen wholly in caricature, in flashes of comic enlargement, but these flashes leave a distinct impression of him, as in the passage in which his face is compared to an imposing but empty parlor. Gloriani, the sculptor who knows the world and is "deluged with orders" (107), is firmly drawn, and is the expert witness of Roderick's innocence and ruin that the novel requires. In Sam Singleton, one sees a very fine discrimination in James's treatment between satire and compassion. After Roderick has spent a disastrous summer at Baden-Baden, misled by a number of young women, Singleton remarks to Mallet that Baden-Baden is in the Black Forest, where one may make "capital" studies of trees. With a smile, and laying "an almost paternal hand" on the little artist's shoulder, Mallet replies: "Unhappily, trees are not Roderick's line" (145). This humorous moment is typical of the sureness of touch that James has at his disposal in rendering the minor figures, who provide the novel with a social background without distracting from the more prominent role of the major characters.

It is partly through the contrast he makes with these sparely depicted minor characters, with circumscribed natures and roles, that Roderick Hudson achieves size. With Roderick, however, James faced certain difficulties in characterization that he was not entirely able to overcome. In his preface to the novel for the New York Edition, James himself comments on the problem created by such a hero. He remarks that Roderick's disintegration occurs too rapidly: "at the rate at which he falls to pieces, he seems to place himself beyond our understanding and our sympathy." Moreover, that Christina should be the sole agent of his disintegration "fails to commend itself to our sense of truth and proportion."[8] The deeper problem with Roderick, however, is that as a romantic artist and passional male character, he is not felt by James from within; James's apprehension of him is largely intellectual. Even his speech is not quite right, is the generalized speech (shaded with refinements of diction and other indications of Anglo-Saxon "breeding") belonging to no one in particular. Roderick is a character one is forced to take on trust, accepting James's word for it that he is a romantic genius and is damned; and he is always an idea.

Another character James fails to "feel" is Mary Garland. She remains wooden, and consequently Rowland's being in love with her does not seem entirely credible. But if Mary Garland has no heart beat, Christina does; she has been endowed with a strongly felt life, and is the most richly created character in the novel. The novel cannot even contain her, for she appears again, in a large way, and with Madame Grandoni as her chaperon, in *The Princess Casamassima* (1886). With her dark or "dusky" hair and implied threat to men, she is a rendering in full dimension of the "dark ladies" who haunt James's early stories. She surpasses all of them in her complexity, her capricious impulses and inner intensity, her rather considerable strength as well as her vulnerability. She is depicted as an actress-in-life, and nothing is at last sacred to her but her self-dramatization. Her conversion to Catholicism in the course of the novel is a *coup de théâtre*, calculated in its effect. Similarly calculated and theatrical is her breaking off her engagement to the prince. "She had played the great scene," James comments when the broken engagement is made known, "she had made her point, and now she had her eye at the hole in the curtain and she was watching the house!" (410).

Beautiful and yet "corrupt" by her own admission, Christina is associated with Europe itself; despite her partly American ancestry, it is Europe that has made her what she is, has embued her with a longing for purity and sublimity, yet destined her to be bartered for coin in the European marketplace. In a melodramatic scene she is compelled to marry the prince, or have her illegitimate birth exposed, but she acquiesces really, although she can hardly admit it and despises herself for it, because she is pledged in an inmost way to the Casamassimas of the world. Her affair with Roderick has, in part, the mythic dimension of a moral encounter between Europe and America, since Roderick, with his indigenous name of Hudson, his innocence and infatuation with "bigness" and abstraction, represents America as much as Christina stands for Europe. He is corrupted by Christina specifically, but through her by the long Roman past, by Europe itself.

Although her motivation and psychology are accounted for

realistically, Christina is given a romantic heightening, particularly in the perverse fascination she exercises. She is associated with forces beyond rational containment—with magic, spells, and enchantments. Madame Grandoni refers to her as "a veritable sorceress" (373), and her poodle (so ornamentally sheared and bedecked with ribbons as to seem a perverse fusion of the natural and the artificial) is "necromantic" (373). When she first appears at Roderick's studio, Roderick exclaims: "Talk of the devil and you see his horns!" (149), and at various times she is evoked as a kind of she-devil. Even the moderate Rowland feels her "spell." "The impression remained," he meditates, ". . . that she was unsafe; that she was a complex, wilful, passionate creature who might easily draw down a too confiding spirit into some strange underworld of unworthy sacrifice, not unfurnished with traces of others of the lost" (186).

Christina is an enchantress in more than aura, since she tempts Roderick to his undoing in very specific episodes of the novel. When she appears at the gathering where Mary Garland is present, she makes an astonishing appearance, dressed in a "burnouse"; and soon after, when he learns that she has broken her engagement to the prince, Roderick is seen in a Buddhist-like or visionary trance, as he lies blissfully on a sofa inhaling the fragrance of a white rose, heedless of his responsibilities to others, or of where his infatuation is taking him. In the scene in the Colosseum, by a mere glance, she puts the idea into Roderick's mind to scale a steep wall in order to pluck a flower for her from a crannied niche, an exploit that would lead, were he to lose his footing, to his plunging into an abyss on the far side of the wall. In this scene, Roderick loses his faculties of judgment, and he does so again at the end when Christina, once more by a mere glance, renews her spell over him, and he can no longer think of his art, work, or responsibilities.

But Roderick and Christina are not merely character opposites, studies in contrast, victimizer and victim. In many essentials, they are very much alike. Christina has a histrionic nature, but Roderick, in some ways, also suggests the stage. On his first appearance in Northampton, he wears a white linen suit, bright red cravat, yellow kid gloves, and "one of those slouched sombreros which are the traditional property of the Virginian or Carolinian of romance" (24). These "rich accessories" (24) imply his nature, his tendency to become a dramatist of his own emotions. His bravura speech at the end is highly self-conscious. Speaking of himself in the past tense, he exclaims: "Say he trembled in every nerve with a sense of beauty and sweetness of life; say he rebelled and protested and struggled; say he was buried alive, with his eyes wide open and his heart beating to madness" (466). He seems conscious above all in this passage of the aesthetic "picture" he makes; his dramatizing of himself reaches toward melodramatizing, with a consequent loss of a proportioned self of reality. Christina, too, is impelled toward the dramatically pictorial, toward a highly styled and self-conscious sense of gesture and moment; and ultimately neither Roderick nor Christina is able to see far beyond themselves.

Roderick and Christina are both self-divided personalities, urged toward an ideal of sublimity but constantly deflected from it by their refusal of discipline. Both divorce the aesthetic from the moral, and insist on an absolute freedom that, being nonreferential, placing them in no real relation to others, becomes a form of enslavement. In the Faustian motif of the novel, their insistence on freedom, self-gratification, and pleasure, marks them out for "damnation." Muttering "damnation" at the end, Roderick tells his mother: "I've gone utterly to the devil!" (424); and his words are almost identical to those of Christina when, late in the work, she tells Mallet: "You remember I told you that I was in part the world's and the devil's. Now they've taken me all" (492–93). The sense that they have not only shared natures but also shared fates is particularly evident at the end. Roderick comes to recognize ultimately that with the loss of purpose in his life his existence is intolerable; and Christina, when she is last seen and looks "tragical," understands that her life with the prince will be a form of prolonged misery. Both characters, who have lived only for themselves, are at last made to confront the futility of their lives.

The Paired Protagonists—Roderick and Rowland

Rowland has been placed in an antithetical relation to Roderick as a character who is rational as Roderick is passionate, and it is partly through him that Roderick's moral failure is kept before the reader. Rowland is a commentator upon and critic of Roderick throughout the work, and has been characterized by Richard Poirier in the following way: "Rowland is pre-eminently sane and reasonable, and he is above all selfless. His selflessness is apparent in his desire to help others, and he is clearly self-sacrificing in his attempts to preserve the engagement of Roderick and Mary, even though he is in love with her."[9] Poirier's interpretation of Rowland as a selfless character set off in contrast to Roderick, who is all self, may seem plausible, but is quite misleading; it fails to search deeply into Rowland's character, and there is much in the relationship of the two men it leaves out of account.

Rowland and Roderick are meant to be closely linked. They have first names beginning with the same letter, and Rowland's last name, Mallet, a sculptor's tool, deepens the impression that they somehow have a common identity. They share in the same "experiment" or project abroad, Roderick creating works of art and Rowland, through him, creating a "life"; and they are constantly together in Europe. It might also be noted that they are both characterized through their heredity. Roderick's father was a Southerner, a man of a rather romantic style who drank himself to death and squandered his fortune, while his mother, on the other hand, is a close-grained New Englander. These two quite different parents prepare for Roderick's conflict—his romantic extravagance and the gnawings of conscience that will not allow him to enjoy his pleasure. But James is equally emphatic in depicting Rowland in the context of a conflicted heredity. Rowland's father, an inhabitant of Hawthorne's Salem, was "a chip of the primal Puritan block, . . . a man of an icy smile and a stony frown" (9). There is in Rowland, as the result of having such a father and austere upbringing, a tendency to recoil from close personal relationships, to nurture his conscience over his pleasures, to "observe" rather than to participate. A complication exists in his heredity, however, since his mother's father was a certain Captain Rowland, a seafaring man whose life was not known wholly to his fellow townspeople, and who, very unexpectedly, went abroad to find a wife. A sabbath-breaker with a taste for relaxed worldly pleasures, Captain Roland makes Rowland's own heritage less sturdy than it might otherwise seem. Like Roderick, Rowland is described as a mixture of the aesthetic and the moral, and he, too, reveals an inner complication or conflict.

In his preface, James dwells on his conception of Rowland and makes rather large claims for him. "My subject," he remarks, ". . . in spite of the title of the book, [was] not directly, in the least, my young sculptor's adventure. This it had been but indirectly, being all the while in essence and in final effect another man's, his friend's and patron's view and experience of him. . . . The centre of interest throughout 'Roderick' is in Rowland Mallet's consciousness, and the drama is the very drama of that consciousness."[10] Rowland does not have the kind of centrally focused consciousness seen later in Lambert Strether in *The Ambassadors*, but he was clearly intended to be more than a marginal figure, or a mere reflector, in his decency, upon Roderick's failings.

Rowland's almost certain evolution from Hawthorne's Miles Coverdale in *The Blithedale Romance* is itself a clue to his inner conflicts. *The Blithedale Romance* is set in New England rather than abroad, but it deals, as *Roderick Hudson* does also, with a noble experiment, an attempt to achieve a new personal enlargement. In Hawthorne's romance, the experiment is conducted in the countryside beyond Boston, evoked in the imagery of a "golden age" of pleasure and possibility, and it is at times made to seem reminiscent of Eden. In this pastoral setting, a fall is enacted, or rather many falls occur, since the characters display an ego involvement so profound as to cancel out any possibility of self-transcendence. The passionate Zenobia and the monomaniac reformer Hollingsworth occupy the foreground, but Coverdale, the "observer," is implicated in their drama. His egotism, although more covert than theirs, is quite as real and his failure is as great. His masked aggressions, failure to commit himself to the ideals he would otherwise like to embrace, and desolate self-involvement at the end, all prepare for Rowland's experience.

When Rowland first appears in Northampton, he tells Cecilia that he would like to be ardent and passionate about something, to undertake a project that would take him out of himself. His adoption of Roderick as a gifted protégé, an artist of potential genius, is to be the absorbing mission through which he will find transcendence and, as he says, "happiness." He will provide Roderick with the means to do what he could not do by himself, to establish himself in Rome and to develop his gifts. In making possible the enlargement of this talented individual, he will also, through the works of art Roderick creates, benefit his fellowmen. Yet even at the beginning, some doubt is cast on Rowland's character and motivation. He says that he wants to feel with an ardor, a passion; but Cecilia wonders if he can really "trust" his inspirations, carry them through. Rowland had once been attracted to Cecilia herself, but by the opening of the novel his romantic interest in her has already faded. The question is subtly raised as to how much of Rowland's interest in taking up Roderick is mere curiosity to see what will happen to him in Europe, an unwarranted tampering with his life. James speaks in an early passage of "sacrificing the faculty of reverence" to a "need for amusement" (25), and although these lines do not refer to Rowland directly, they are intended to raise a certain kind of doubt about him.

The Temptation and Fall of Rowland Mallet

Rowland's attraction to Mary Garland complicates his relationship to Roderick even before they leave Northampton, and this complication deepens when they go abroad. In Rome, when Rowland sees "the young sculptor's day pass in a single sustained flight," James writes, ". . . he felt a pang of some envious pain" (99). Rowland's envy of what Roderick possesses and he does not includes Mary Garland. Rowland may seem sane and moderate, forbearing and generous; but as his trait of envy indicates, he is far from perfect; and as the novel progresses his character is tested. After Christina has reappeared in Rome and begun to show an interest in Roderick, Rowland attends a ball at which she asks him about Roderick's life in New England, wishing to know particularly if there is a young woman in his life. At this point, Rowland has been brooding over his suppressed desire for Mary Garland, feeling resentment toward Roderick in possessing her. Before answering Christina he hesitates, then tells her that Roderick has, indeed, a fiancée in Northampton, a most admirable young woman. Rowland's indiscretion in revealing the existence of Roderick's fiancée is perhaps marginal, since the engagement has been announced, and Roderick may himself tell Christina of it. Yet his telling her of Mary Garland *is* a lapse in Rowland's mission to ensure Roderick's safety abroad. Rowland must know, at some level, that he is inviting Christina's interest in Roderick, for she would certainly be piqued by the prospect of taking him away from this young woman, if only to prove that she could. In that eventuality, too, Mary Garland would be unlikely to marry Roderick.

The conflict in Rowland between his duty to Roderick, and his resentment of him and desire for his fiancée, deepens in the course of the novel. After Christina announces her engagement to the prince and Roderick is rapidly deteriorating, Rowland takes a trip by himself to Florence, where, visiting the Pitti Palace, he feels mocked by the serenity and unattainable respose of Raphael's paintings. His own repose has been shaken by the apparent failure of his enterprise abroad, and feeling aggrieved and resentful, he desires something *personal* out of the experience, a tangible gain. The idea of "compensation in concrete form . . . shaped itself . . . into the image of Mary Garland" (313), and in his mind Rowland dreams Roderick's death:

For forty-eight hours there swam before Rowland's eyes a vision of the wondrous youth, graceful and beautiful as he passed, plunging like a diver into a misty gulf. The gulf was destruction, annihilation, death; but if death had been decreed, why shouldn't the agony be at least brief? Beyond this vision there faintly glimmered another. . . . It

represented Mary Garland standing there with eyes in which the horror seemed slowly, slowly to expire, and hanging motionless hands
which at last made no resistance when his own offered to take them.
When of old a man was burnt at the stake it was cruel to have to be
present; but one's presence assumed, it was charity to lend a hand,
to pile up the fuel and make the flames do their work quickly and
the smoke muffle up the victim. And it didn't diminish the charity
that this was perhaps an obligation especially felt if one had a re-
versionary interest in something the victim was to leave behind.
(314–15)

Deeply troubled by this vision of his piling up fuel while Roderick is burned at the stake, Rowland goes into the countryside
to ease his mind; and there he visits a Franciscan convent, poised
precariously on a hillside above a "nakedly romantic gorge" (316).
In the convent's terraced garden, he drives "the devil" from his
thoughts, the impulse to speed Roderick along to his ruin. The
setting of this temptation is itself full of implication, since the
"gorge" at the convent's edge is a reminder of the misty gulf into
which he has imagined Roderick plunging, and of the "abyss" on
the far side of the Colosseum wall into which Roderick had nearly
fallen while attempting to obtain a wildflower for Christina. Roderick dies, in fact, by a plunge into a ravine, and this foreshadowing imagery implies a complicity between Rowland and Christina
in his death.

Rowland does not succumb to his temptation in the convent
garden, but his testing continues on beyond this scene. Later in
the work, after Christina has married the prince, Roderick announces that he is willing to return to Northampton. He will not
necessarily find peace there, but he may, under the stabilizing influence of his mother, Mary Garland, and familiar surroundings,
removed from his turmoil in Rome, find a kind of reconciliation
to his circumstances. A bust of his mother that he has lately made,
a work quite unlike the romantic abstractions he has previously
sought to embody in marble, suggests that his life and career may
still be salvaged; in the chastening implied in the bust, which is
perfectly unflattered and yet admirably tender, a work accomplished

with "the most unerring art" (362), there is some indication that
he may even have grown. Yet at this very point, Rowland advises him to remain in Italy for another year in order to prove
himself, and prevails upon him to spend the summer in Europe
at least. Now why should Rowland do this? The point has clearly
been reached for Roderick to return to America, and he is ready to.
Rowland's motives become clearer when one notices that in this
same section Roderick begins to undergo a change of attitude
toward Mary Garland; begins to become reconciled to a life with
her in Northampton; a life that would not be excited with passion,
like his affair with Christina, but quite possibly be what he most
needs. Rowland may be sincere in his desire to see Roderick pull
himself together in Europe, but it is also apparent that were
Roderick to leave at that point, he himself would have no hope of
ever having Mary Garland.

Rowland's motives are the more suspect when one considers
that he must, although he cannot know when or where it will
occur, have some prevision of Christina's reappearing. And he
must know that such a meeting would have unsettling and possibly fateful consequences for his friend. The impression of Rowland's betrayal of his friend is heightened, moreover, by Roderick's
pointedly telling him in this section how much he feels he can
always "trust" him, and how much he now absolutely relies on
him. He even remarks that without him he could not go on. But
in this same section, Rowland's fingers itch "to handle forbidden
fruit" (475), and when Christina does appear again, reducing
Roderick to an unreasoning infatuation, so that he borrows money
not only from Rowland but even from Mary Garland in order
to pursue her, Rowland can barely stifle his "joy." In their final
scene together, Rowland and Roderick fall into an argument, and
Rowland is at last provoked into admitting that he himself has
all the while been in love with Mary Garland. In pointing out his
own "self sacrifice" to Roderick in this way, Rowland contributes
to his death. In a disturbed state of mind, realizing now that he
stands in Rowland's way with Mary, unable to repay his great debt
to him, twitted by him about his own sacrifice of himself, Roderick

"sacrifices" himself in his plunge into the Alpine ravine. Christina more overtly, Rowland in fine, subtle ways, act together to put Roderick to death. Roderick is their "sacrificial goat," their sacrificed ideal.

The Ending

In the last view of Roderick as he lies dead in the ravine, "fallen from a great height" (523), attention is called to his astonishing beauty; and his beauty in death is a reminder of the beauty that he might have brought into the world through his art. The experiment abroad was undertaken in the name of an ennobling ideal, requiring self-abnegation, devotion, and faith; but in one way or another, the principal characters of the novel are all unable to meet the requirements of such faith, and no ideal is realized. In no case does this failure of fidelity to a proposed ideal bring the characters involved any "happiness." At the beginning, Rowland remarks that he is tired of himself, his own thoughts, own affairs, own eternal company. "True happiness, we are told," he remarks, "consists in getting out of one's self" (7); and Christina says almost exactly the same thing: "I'm tired to death of myself; I would give all I possess to get out of myself" (203). And what Roderick's "damnation" really means is suggested near the end when he cries: "I am fit only to be alone" (513). Roderick fails of transcendence, Christina is condemned to the torment of her self-enclosure, and Rowland is confronted with blank walls and doors that do not open to him. Roderick was Rowland's great opportunity for self-enlargement, the one character through whom he might have found the "key" he needed to enter life. Near the end, following the argument between Rowland and Roderick that sends Roderick to his death, Rowland realizes that he has lost his keys near the place where he had spoken to Roderick. He cannot find these keys, and in Northampton, he exclaims: "I spend my days groping for the latch of a closed door" (8). The drama of potentiality ended in failure, Mary Garland unwilling to have him, Rowland sees himself doomed to go on forever futilely "observing."

Somewhat studious and stiff-jointed, *Roderick Hudson* is nevertheless a mature and intricately designed "first" novel that rewards many readings. All of James's preoccupations are in it—innocence and violation, the betrayal theme, Europe and America, the artist, and art as moral analogue. Like *Watch and Ward*, a fable or morality can be detected in its inner story. But unlike the apprenticeship work, it is a fully achieved work of art in which a sophisticated novel of manners and romance are successfully merged. If *Watch and Ward* is an awkward prophecy, *Roderick Hudson*, published only four years later, is a partial realization of that prophecy, the point at which James arrives as a novelist.

Chapter Four

The American: Innocence Abroad

Background

Genesis and Text.   James's six months spent in New York City in 1875 involved him in almost ceaseless writing activity; in that brief time he not only completed *Roderick Hudson* but also published a large number of reviews and essays.[1] Such relentless work does not suggest that James found much in New York City, of a social nature, to "enjoy"; and when an opportunity soon presented itself that would enable him to return to Europe, he immediately took advantage of it. The opportunity came about when Whitelaw Reid, publisher of the *New York Tribune*, offered him an assignment as a Paris correspondent, contributing regular columns on the city's social and cultural life, to begin about October, 1875. In October James left for Europe, and by the following month had settled in Paris. Thereafter twenty of his columns appeared in the *Tribune*, from November, 1875, to August, 1876,[2] before being discontinued by mutual agreement between James and the paper. James had eventually been asked by Reid to write his columns more nearly on the level of journalism, which he refused to do.

Soon after arriving, James called for the first time on Turgenev, whose work he warmly admired, and an important literary friendship began—with Turgenev, at fifty-seven, near the end of his career, and James, at thirty-two, still at an early stage of his. Turgenev, in turn, introduced James to Flaubert, then in his middle fifties, at his apartment in the Faubourg St. Honoré, where he also met Flaubert's circle that included Edmond de Goncourt, Emile Zola, Alphonse Daudet, and Guy de Maupassant. James's introduction to this cenacle of French naturalists would be one of his enduring impressions of his year in Paris. But *The American*, which he was soon to write, had little in common with their sense of life, which, to him, seemed narrow or cynical.

In one respect, James's stay in Paris had something in common with Christopher Newman's experience of it in the novel. After crossing the Atlantic, he proclaimed to his family: "I take possession of the old world—I inhale it—I appropriate it!"[3] Yet in his letters of that year, he complains of his limited access to Parisian life, his failure to penetrate very far beyond the city's small, enclosed American colony; and his columns to the *Tribune* continually suggest a spectator-outsider. In *The American*, Newman also has an imperious desire to take possession of Europe that is thwarted by the nature of French customs, which work against a ready acceptance of outsiders. Yet it would be misleading to suggest that James found no acceptance in France at all, for he did make new acquaintances and form new associations. Some of those he met at that time, in fact, find their way, in fictional form, into the novel. Paul Zhukovsky, an amiable expatriate and dilettante painter, became a close companion, and inspired the conception of Valentin de Bellegarde, the close friend of Newman's. The Edward Lee Childes, an American couple who were close friends of the Nortons, suggested the idea of the Tristrams. Even the "fat duchess," a character who seems wholly imaginary, was based on James's glimpse of an actual person, the princess of Saxe-Coburg.[4]

James appears to have intended from the beginning to use his experience in Paris as the basis for a novel. Soon after his arrival, in fact, in late November, 1875, he contacted F. P. Church, editor of *The Galaxy*, proposing to write a serial novel with a Parisian setting for the magazine. When negotiations with *The Galaxy* fell through, James had *The Galaxy* send the first installments of the novel to Howells, who accepted it for the *Atlantic. The American* began its serialization in the *Atlantic* in June, 1876, and ran through twelve issues, assuring James of an income of $1,350— an ample amount on which to live while the novel was being written. Despite its unhappy ending, which Howells opposed, *The American* proved to be the most popular work James had thus far produced;[5] and later, in 1890, he adapted it for the London stage, where it enjoyed a modest success.[6] The serialized version of *The American* was revised for style when it appeared in book form in 1877, and other minimal revisions were made for the first English book edition of 1879. Revisions for the New York Edition (1907–9), however, were extensive—so much so that the original and final versions represent almost two "different" works. The 1907 version makes Newman somewhat older, more sophisticated and self-conscious, and by doing so muffles the comedy that makes the original version attractive. For freshness and immediacy, the original version of *The American* is the one generally preferred.

Source and Influence. In his preface to *The American* for the New York Edition, James recalls how the idea for the novel first came to him. "I was seated in an American 'horse-car,'" he writes, "when I found myself of a sudden, considering... as the theme of a 'story,' the situation in another country, and an aristo-cratic society, of some robust but insidiously beguiled and betrayed, some cruelly wronged, compatriot; the point being... that he should suffer at the hands of persons pretending to represent the highest possible civilization and to be of an order in every way superior to his own." He goes on to explain that in time the American would arrive at his "just vindication," and then "would fail of all triumphantly and all vulgarly enjoying it." He would hold his revenge and cherish it, but in the very moment of forcing it home "would sacrifice it in disgust, the bitterness of his personal loss yielding to the very force of his aversion."[7]

The inspiration for the novel may well have come to him in New York, while he was completing *Roderick Hudson*, but even before that time a foreshadowing of the plot can be noticed in

James's story "Guest's Confession" (1872), in which the narrator destroys an incriminating document rather than to use it for coercive purposes. "Guest's Confession" anticipates *The American* also in the character of Crawford, a Westerner who dimly forecasts the "type" of Newman. Resembling Newman physically, Crawford is "a tall, lean gentleman, on the right side of forty," with a "clear blue eye, in which simplicity and shrewdness contended." James describes him as a "genial sceptic": "If he disbelieved much that he saw, he believed everything he fancied, and for a man who had seen much of the rougher and baser side of life, he was able to fancy some very gracious things of men, to say nothing of women." Moreover, Crawford, like Newman, after many adventures in the American West, has scaled the ladder of fortune, and is now ready to select a wife.

But this somewhat crude story of the early 1870s merely provides hints for the novel. Christopher Newman's heroic size and vitality are suggested by other sources, particularly by American folklore, as Constance Rourke has pointed out in her book *American Humor.* She notes that Newman, in his physical appearance and independent attitude, belongs unmistakably to an American, indeed, a Yankee tradition. He is a combination of innocence and shrewdness belonging to Yankee fables and stage plays like *Our American Cousin,* in which the Yankee is a strongly typed figure of comic potentialities. Even Newman's name has the faintly comic symbolism of a line of heroes, like Jedidiah Homebred, who appear in Yankee fables. Yet Newman's local origins are never given; and if the folklore of the Yankee clings to him, he partakes, too, of the folklore of the West. The Pacific Coast had been the scene of his financial successes. "He might have been in San Francisco or Virginia City with Mark Twain," Rourke writes, "he had the habits of the time and place."

Newman's association with Twain and the Western humorists is evident when James remarks that he "had sat with western humorists in knots, round cast-iron stoves, and seen 'tall' stories grow taller without toppling over, and his own imagination had learned the trick of piling up consistent wonders" (97).[8] James would have had reason to be conscious of Twain, since *Roderick Hudson* was serialized side by side in the *Atlantic* with Twain's *Old Times on the Mississippi*—the very time when James first conceived *The American*. Moreover, Twain's *The Innocents Abroad* (1869), a popular success of considerable proportions, had established the type of comic encounter between the irreverent American Westerner and European culture. *The Innocents Abroad* makes Newman plausible as he appears at the opening in the Louvre, preferring copies of the old masterpieces to their originals—just as Twain had remarked that he "could not help noticing how superior the copies were to the original."

But the situation in which Newman is placed is indebted to Turgenev, particularly to his novel *A Nest of Gentlefolk* (1858), with its theme of frustration and failure. Lavretsky, the hero of *A Nest of Gentlefolk*, does not "belong" in the circle in which he appears, falls in love with "the rarest bird in the nest," and after a series of complications stands powerlessly by while Lisa enters a convent. In Turgenev's gently melancholic ending, Lavretsky returns to the convent in a mute farewell, just as, in a late scene in *The American* having a similar atmosphere of melancholy, Newman returns for a last view of the convent in which Claire de Cintré will be closed up for life. The contrasts Turgenev works with (the rising "new" class versus the "old" gentry class); the way in which his characters "belong" to their peculiar backgrounds and are representative of them; the assumption of mutual "happiness" in the relationship of the lovers that is shown to rest on illusion; the theme of aspiration and failure focused by the final scene at the convent—all of these features of Turgenev's novel are influential on *The American*.

Other influences, however, play over the work. During his year in Paris, James went frequently to the Théâtre Français, and he was steeped at this time in the work of the French dramatists—particularly Scribe and Sardou, Dumas, *fils*, and Augier. In one of several references at that time to his saturation in the French theater, James wrote to his brother William: "I know the Theatre Français by heart."[9] The opening chapters of the novel are conceived as "scenes," in which characters make distinct entrances and exits, and in which the Salon Carré of the Louvre itself has the effect of a stage set. Later episodes involving Newman and Mrs. Tristram are set in drawing rooms and are strongly scenic in their effect; and, generally, scenic form is more conspicuous if not more pervasive in *The American* than in *Roderick Hudson.*

It might also be noted that the romantic melodrama of the later part of the novel borrows from popular literature of the day; the concealed murder, incriminating document, and old retainer able to reveal the skeleton in the family closet, have affinities with both the French stage and popular Victorian fiction. More specifically, James's sketching of the noble French family with a guilty past strongly suggests the influence of George Sand. In June, 1876, while he was approximately midway through the novel, James learned of Sand's death and wrote a memorial to her in one of his letters to the *Tribune*; and during this same period he reviewed her career as a novelist in a lengthy essay that was included in *French Poets and Novelists*. James's reimmersion in Sand's fiction accounts for the romantic stylization of the later part of *The American*, a device by which James also attempts to throw dust in his reader's eyes, to conceal the fact that his personal knowledge of the French nobility was meager indeed—was almost purely literary. James's failure of direct observation in this section, however, is partly understandable. During his year in Paris, he was, after all, as he recalled five years later, "an eternal outsider."[10]

The Fairy-Tale Element

The American resembles *Roderick Hudson* in having been cast partly in the form of a fairy tale. In the opening of *Roderick Hudson*, Mary Garland exclaims to Rowland that his appearance in Northampton is "like a fairy tale . . . your coming here all unannounced, unknown, so rich and so polite, and carrying off my cousin in a golden cloud." With a similar evocation of romance, in the opening scene set in Rome, the belvedered roof of the casino of the Villa Ludovisi makes Roderick think of the prospect "from a

castle turret in a fairy-tale." Almost immediately, a young woman
of astonishing beauty appears and is likened to a "princess," which
she literally becomes by the end. The prince who claims her has
a fabulous background, is the scion of a princely house six hundred
years old, and has a palatial home with a marbled terrace four
hundred feet long. "Stupendous!" Christina exclaims of it. "To go
from one end to the other the Prince must have out his golden
coach." Christina herself belongs to fairy tale—with her preter-
naturally radiant beauty, her fatal aura, her power of enchantment.
As a fairy-tale princess, she is played off against Roderick, "the
young Prince of the Belle-Arti." When Roderick lies asleep on the
wooded grounds of the Villa Mandragone, Christina appears suddenly to awaken him; and as she does, James refers, with an ironic
reversal of sexual roles, to the fairy tale of Sleeping Beauty in the
Wood. But the wonder to which Christina awakens the sleeping
Roderick is the destruction of his gifts. After his involvement with
the terrible princess, no magic, "no waving of any blest wand," can
restore his creative powers.

In *The American*, another princess of fairy tale appears. Claire
de Cintré belongs to a noble French family "of fabulous antiquity"
(46), dating back to some time before the ninth century; and
when Newman visits her at the Bellegarde house in the Faubourg
St. Germain, she seems to him "enveloped in a sort of fantastic
privacy" (81) that gives her a fairy-tale rarity. At the Bellegardes'
ball, Mme. d'Outreville remarks: "But your real triumph, my dear
sir, is pleasing the countess; she is as difficult as a princess in a
fairy tale. Your success is a miracle" (190). At the same ball Newman is said to resemble the bear in the fairy tale of Beauty and
the Beast. And elsewhere Claire recounts a fairy tale to her young
niece of the young prince who marries the "beautiful Florabella,"
and carries her off to live with him in the land of the Pink Sky.

Newman himself, whose whim is a *"caprice de prince"* (35),
also steps out of a fabled background. His wealth (unspecified but
apparently in the millions) gives him the stature of a merchant
prince, and underlies the sense he has of illimitable possibilities in
life. But he is impressive, too, in the way his wealth was made—

from nothing, and seemingly with effortless ease. It is no wonder that many of the characters in the novel are "fascinated by New-man's plain prose version of the legend of El Dorado" (204), and that other legends of larger-than-life size attach to him. One of Mme. de Bellegarde's guests tells him: "Oh, you have your *legende*. We have heard that you have had a career the most checkered, the most *bizarre* ... and are ... fabulously rich" (189). Like a giant of fable, he is said to "walk in seven-league boots" (181). It is fitting, therefore, that he should aspire to marry Claire de Cintré, a fairy-tale princess, the rarest treasure of the old world.

The Use of Romance

The evocation of fairy tale gives *The American* a large, ro-mantic heightening. But romance is also present in the work in James's use of romantic melodrama, particularly in the later part. One may distinguish between James's accomplished use of fairy tale and his use of romantic melodrama, which damages the work considerably. It is part of James's reliance on melodrama that Claire should have a "wicked old mother" (78); and an older brother whose devotion to formality and tradition have turned him almost to stone; and that their villainy near the end should be revealed by Mrs. Bread. To Newman, she relates the story of how the old marquis was murdered, in effect, by his wife who, when he was dying, put his medicine out of reach. Her stare, in a manner suggesting the Gothic mode, was the death instrument: "It was like a frost on flowers" (267).

In this later section, James resorts increasingly to melodramatic conventions. The villainous deed, for example, takes place off stage. Incredibly, a witness survives, and even holds a damning document, written in the marquis's own hand. Valentin's fatal duel and the scene in which the Bellegardes force Claire to renounce her engagement to Newman seem creakingly contrived. Claire's renunciation is curiously unreal, because one feels that the pres-sures on her occurring in these shrouded circumstances are specious, have not been imagined by James himself. James's treatment of Claire in the final part belongs not only to a melodramatic but even to a Gothic convention. The country house of the Bellegardes at Fleurières might have come out of Edgar Allan Poe: a chateau said to be crumbling with age, its dull brick walls and time-darkened cupolas are mirrored in the still water of a moat before it, as if the house were held under an evil enchantment. When Newman enters this melancholy residence, he is received by Claire, who wears a black dress and is depicted in images of darkness. There is a "monastic rigidity in her dress" (238), and her touch is "portentously lifeless" (238). In committing herself to the convent of the Carmelite nuns, she will be "buried alive," will "muffle herself in ascetic rags and entomb herself" (244). The idea of a living entombment, which belongs markedly to Gothicism, becomes operatic when Newman returns to the convent, located on the Rue d'Enfer, to hear the strange chant of the nuns, their only human utterance, that becomes "a wail and a dirge" (277).

In his preface, James discusses *The American* as if it were to be regarded almost entirely as a romance. "The balloon of experience," he remarks, "is in fact of course tied to the earth, and under that necessity we swing, thanks to a rope of remarkable length, in the more or less commodious car of the imagination; but it is by the rope we know where we are, and from the moment that cable is cut, we are at large and unrelated."[11] The art of the romancer, he continues, is to "cut the cable," and that is what it seems to him, in retrospect, he has done in *The American*. What makes the statement peculiar are the words "much to my surprise and after long years," as if he had not made this recognition while writing the novel. The reader is left wondering how a writer of James's sophistication could not have known he was writing romance at the time.

In the preface, he concedes weaknesses in the work that result from its romance mode—"the queer falsity of the Bellegardes." They would not have acted in life, James remarks, as they are represented as having acted in the novel. They would not have rejected Newman, but would have taken him and his money eagerly, and would then have adjusted themselves to the situation as quietly as possible. This observation seems right, but it does not explain why James had not made it in 1876. The preface leaves many questions unanswered; and it is also misleading in suggesting that *The American* may be seen wholly as romance. The novel contains much realistic observation, and certain characters in it are presented realistically. Others, like the Bellegarde mother and elder son, belong to a romance mode partly, and partly to a realistic one, but to neither fully.

Characters in the Dimension of Realism

Noémie Nioche, one of James's notable successes in the novel, belongs entirely to realism. As a French adventuress, or woman who rises from a lower to a higher social class through her sexual wiles, she has a convincing typicality. There is no romance vagueness about her; she is firmly "placed," and is played off against Claire de Cintré, who belongs distinctively to an aristocratic order of large exclusions and determined privacy. Noémie's life, by contrast, has a "public" nature. She puts herself on display at the Louvre, ostensibly working as a copyist but actually waiting to meet a gentleman who will advance her fortunes. At the end, she is on display in London's Hyde Park, on the arm of Lord Deepmere.

Noémie is flanked by her parent, who is also drawn realistically, and often with comic irony. Seen at the beginning, he is reminiscent of the Cavaliere Giacosa in *Roderick Hudson*. "M. Nioche," James comments,

wore a glossy wig, of an unnatural colour, which overhung his little meek, white, vacant face and left it hardly more expressive than the unfeatured block upon which these articles are displayed in the barber's window. He was an exquisite image of shabby gentility.... Among other things M. Nioche had lost courage. Adversity had not only ruined him, it had frightened him, and he was evidently going through his remnant of life on tiptoe for fear of waking up the hostile fates. (22)

With his darned gloves and desperately brushed coat, M. Nioche attempts to keep up appearances, although not very successfully, for it is clear from his first appearance that the inner spring of his being has been broken. Even at the beginning, he is compromised by Noémie, who foists him upon Newman as a language tutor (for which he is too generously paid), although his command of English is at best uncertain. At the end, as he follows meekly after Noémie while she hobnobs with Deepmere, he is compromised by her wholly.

Lord Deepmere mingles with the Bellegardes at their ball, but he shares none of their romance mystique. A person of "no great range" (161), Deepmere is a short man with a bald head, a short nose, and an upper jaw in which his front teeth are missing; and he laughs a great deal in the manner of a man who is shy, "catching his breath with an odd startling sound, as the most convenient imitation of repose" (161). His physiognomy, James remarks, "denoted great simplicity, a certain amount of brutality, and probable failure in the past to profit by rare educational advantages" (161). Near the end of the novel, in Hyde Park, he admits that his taking up with Noémie, and showing her off in public, may seem "cheeky," since she was responsible for Valentin's death. But he seems no more troubled in conscience, really, than Noémie herself.

Tom Tristram is similar to Lord Deepmere insofar as he implies surface rather than depth. Although he has lived in Paris for six years, he has never entered the Louvre until the day that, acting on a sudden whim and looking vaguely for diversion, he goes in to encounter Newman. An American expatriate type as much as a character, he spends his time at his club, where he shakes "hands all round" (39). His face, James notes, "was not remarkable for intensity of expression, he looked like a person who would willingly shake hands with any one" (26). Mrs. Tristram has been given more characterizing touches than her husband, but she is also a distinctly limited human being. Having been slighted by a clever man, she married a fool to show the "thankless wit" that she had never esteemed him. Restless, discontented, she has some "avidity of imagination" (38), and becomes Newman's confidante, helping to launch his affair with Claire.

Another realistically drawn character, having a sharply limited point of view, is Mr. Babcock, the Unitarian minister from Massachusetts. Unlike Tristram, Mr. Babcock is "earnest"; but he is earnest to a fault. His parishioners have gotten up a purse so that he may travel abroad, and thus improve his culture and ministry. But his conscientious effort to absorb European culture, which is far more a rigorous duty than a pleasure, constantly makes him an outsider to it. With his fretted "moral reaction," he cannot enter into the spirit of culture, and is left perplexed by what he sees. The European temperament itself strikes him as a disturbingly impure mixture of good and bad. Mr. Babcock, James writes, "really knew as little about the bad, in any quarter of the world, as a nursing infant; his most vivid realisation of evil had been the discovery that one of his college classmates who was studying architecture in Paris, had a love affair with a young woman who did not expect him to marry her" (69). In his "moral reaction" and innocence of evil, Babcock might be a neighbor of the Wentworths in *The Europeans*; and he does, in fact, anticipate them. As much as the other subordinate figures, he contributes to the sense of limited or restricted consciousness in the novel's characters.

Theater as Metaphor and Motif

In a number of cases, the characters in the novel are revealed by their relation to dominant motifs, such as that of the theater. Imagery of the theater appears early in the work and continues throughout. James writes that at the Bellegardes' house, Newman "sat by without speaking, looking at the entrances and exits, the greetings and chatterings, of Madame de Cintré's visitors. He felt as if he were at the play, and as if his own speaking would be an interruption; sometimes he wished he had a book, to follow the dialogue" (98). Claire herself becomes an actress on Newman's mental stage. "She was part of the play," James comments, "that he was seeing acted, quite as much as her companions; but how she filled the stage and how much better she did it! . . . It was the mystery—it was what she was off the stage, as it were—that interested Newman most of all" (98). In the opening scene at the Louvre, Noémie is said to have an "aptitude for playing a part at short notice" (20); and when he learns of Newman's plan to have Claire as his wife, Valentin declares that he "shall be actor, so far as I can, as well as spectator" (107). In another scene, Valentin is also depicted as playing a role; James notes that he "was what is called in France a *gentilhomme*, of the purest source, and his rule of life, so far as it was definite, was to play the part of a *gentilhomme*" (92). At the Bellegardes' ball, Newman, too, is said to have "played his part" (186). These numerous allusions create the sense of Newman's experience as having a stagelike unreality. But further than that, they insinuate the illusion of limitless freedom. As spectators to a drama, the characters are free to enjoy the spectacle of others' lives. Yet as participants and actors themselves, they are confined within the drama they witness.

The implication of the theater metaphor becomes clear in the case of Valentin. More than the others, he thinks of life as amusing diversion, and he frequently refers to it in the imagery of his being a spectator at the theater. It is in this way that he regards Mme. Dandelard, a young Italian widow who has recently come to Paris, and will soon be compromised by her new life. "To see this little woman's little drama play itself out, now," he tells Newman, "is for me, an intellectual pleasure" (99). Newman's attempt to win Claire also provides him with a drama that will be "very entertaining." "Excuse my speaking of it in that cold-blooded fashion," he remarks, "but the matter must, of necessity, be for me something of a spectacle. It's positively exciting" (107).

In the early part particularly Valentin regards Noémie as an actress on a social stage, with himself as spectator. He is convinced that, with her perfect heartlessness, she is "one of the celebrities of the future" (135). "This little baggage entertains me" (179), he tells Newman; and again: "Intelligent, determined, ambitious, unscrupulous, capable of looking at a man strangled without changing colour, she is, upon my honour, extremely entertaining"

(179). Yet later, when he becomes infatuated with her, he changes his role from that of amused spectator to involved participant. Before he loses his life he comes to recognize in human terms what Noémie's heartlessness means. In his movement from intellectually entertained spectator to participant who must suffer, Valentin illustrates the difference between surface and depth, between head and heart. James has such a distinction in mind in *The Portrait of a Lady* when Ralph Touchett tells Isabel "you want to see but not to feel."

The Art Metaphor

James's art metaphor is perhaps even more pervasive in the novel than the metaphor of theater. *The American* begins in a great museum of art, and its characters are at times defined by their relationship to art. Mr. Babcock, for example, tells Newman that life and art "seem to me intensely serious things" (72), but he is unable to comprehend art, because his responses to it are always rigidly judgmental, and because he has denied himself the experience that would give art a humanly meaningful context. Noémie is by profession a copyist and is first seen against a background of great masterpieces. But her copies are poor, contain no sincerity, and her relation to art is merely exploitative. The obtuse Tristram declares: "I don't care for pictures; I prefer the reality" (29), revealing that he can establish no relation between art and life. And there is, certainly, no art to his life. Valentin's art-littered apartment suggests his cultivation and collector's passion, but also his tendency toward aimlessness. Urbain de Bellegrade is also revealed by his relation to the fine arts. At dinner with Newman, he utters "some polished aphorism upon the flesh-tints of Rubens and the good-taste of Sansovino" (139). But his allusions to art are intended merely to chill the air, to keep others at a distance from him. His cultivation of art and tradition is coldly sterile.

But it is Newman, most of all, upon whom the art metaphor comments. It is significant that he appears at the beginning in a museum of art, where, after having looked up a great many pictures in his guidebook, he suffers an "aesthetic headache" (17). He is unacquainted with standards, and James remarks that he finds it uncomfortable to square himself with one. Being unformed, he occupies, on the Boulevard Haussmann, a "great gilded parlour" (88) that Valentin compares to a ballroom. When Newman notes his smile, Valentin adds wittily: "It is not size only . . . , but splendour, and harmony, and beauty of detail. It was the smile of admiration" (88). Newman thinks of himself as being a noble fellow, but his mind is vague, and has failed to take in large areas of experience. Hence his discomfiture in the world of art, the disturbing, half-formed recognition that he may not, after all, have a sophisticated view of things. Although supposing himself to be shrewd, he is evoked comically as an American innocent abroad. Tristram tells him: "I suppose you're a smart fellow, eh," and as Newman looks over at some nurses and infants, which "imparted to the scene a kind of primordial, pastoral simplicity" (31), he says that he supposes he is.

Newman's assumptions, like his background, are prototypically American. Benjamin Franklin is alluded to several times in the work, and Newman, like Dr. Franklin, is a self-made man who has risen to considerable success through his enterprise. He assures Claire that she will be "safe" with him, because "energy and ingenuity can arrange everything" (113). In his success, he is encouraged to take a flattering view of himself, and to regard life in terms of material well-being and prosperity. It seems to him as if he had been placed in the world to make money, to wrest a fortune from defiant opportunity. "This idea," James notes, "completely filled his horizon and satisfied his imagination" (32). In Newman consciousness, which James in his preface to *The American* calls "the great extension," is not highly developed. He looks upon experience as an easy, relaxed, and pleasurable self-expansion, an expansion wholly outward. His vision recognizes no limits upon the self. The metaphor he frequently thinks in is the worldly one of money—money, will, and possession. His matrimonial ambitions are expressed in this idiom. "I want," he says, "to possess, in a word, the best article in the market" (44).

In the course of the novel, Newman confronts obstruction, and
the first really irreversible failure of his life. He befriends Valentin,
and by introducing him to Noémie, sends him to his death. He
intrudes upon the Bellegardes and in doing so sends Claire to a
convent, where she will experience a death in life. He himself
suffers, experiences a kind of purgatory, and is at the end a chastened version of the man he had been at the beginning. Newman's
experience is intimated by James through his use of symmetrical
character relationships and by a subplot that comments on the
main one. Valentin and Claire, for example, have been paired:
they resemble each other physically in a striking way, and represent the purer part of the Bellegardes' mixed heritage; and through
his interference Newman brings harm to both. But Newman and
Valentin are also paired. They become inseparable friends, and the
attraction of each to a woman has an unfortunate outcome. But
further, and although they may at first seem quite unlike one another, they reveal natures that are in certain respects surprisingly
similar. With his easy, relaxed attitudes, Valentin looks upon life
as "diversion," and so does Newman in the early part of the work.
"I want to be amused," he declares; "I came to Europe for that"
(86). Only later does he begin to achieve a sense of limits, of context and relation, and of perspective implied by art.

The Relation of Main Plot and Subplot

The main plot of *The American* is made parallel with the
subplot at a number of specific points, and in such a way as to
link the principal characters of each, Newman and Noémie.
Newman's engagement to Claire coincides with Noémie's being
"launched"; and when Newman is exultant over his good fortune,
Noémie has the triumphant feeling that her ideal has been "satisfied." Their feeling of self-satisfaction, however, is followed by
scenes in which others suffer. At the same time that Valentin
leaves for Switzerland to fight his duel, Claire leaves for the
country; and Valentin's death coincides with Claire's decision to
enter the convent. James's use of these parallels implies that

Newman and Noémie at this point have common roles; just as Noémie's self-assertion victimizes Valentin, Newman's victimizes Claire. Newman and Noémie have in common, further, that they are the two "democrats" of the novel, the two intruders into the established order. Like Newman, Noémie is aspiring and confident of her ability to rise, to overcome all obstacles through the assertion of her will. As Newman represents worldly success achieved, Noémie is worldly success anticipated. By the end of the novel, in fact, in the scene in Hyde Park, Noémie has achieved the success to which she has aspired. But the nature of this success comments on what has been wrong all along with Newman's ideal of prosperity and self-gratification. It is a shallow ideal.

Belonging wholly to the world and to its market values, Noémie remarks appropriately at the beginning: "Everything I have is for sale" (133). Her values can be seen in the Louvre when, admiring an ostentatiously dressed woman, Noémie reflects that "to be able to drag such a train over a polished floor was a felicity worth any price" (131). Urbain's wife, highly placed socially but one of the emptiest characters in the novel, a woman compared by James to a cracked perfume bottle, is what Noémie would most like to be. Moreover, in order to realize such an ideal, she is prepared to sacrifice every human value. Valentin says of her: "In one gift—perfect heartlessness—I will warrant she is unsurpassed. She had not as much heart as will go on the point of a needle" (135). In the Hyde Park scene, her heartlessness is suggested again in the same imagery, as her eyes glitter with an impudence "fine as a needle-point" (299). With her intensely narrowed concentration upon herself alone, her consciousness is minute.

By the end, Noémie becomes a kind of parody of Newman's early values—money, will, and power, the assumption that the world exists to give pleasure to one's self. In his relationship with Claire, he discovers a world outside the self, and in doing so comes to the brink of spiritual awareness. In the main plot, Newman fails to possess his ideal materially, while in the subplot Noémie succeeds fully in realizing hers. But the contrast they make merely emphasizes the valuelessness of Noémie's success. One might say that Noémie fails through success, while Newman succeeds through failure, achieving a new integrity at the end in the face of outward defeat.

The Inner Story

Newman's experience in Paris is framed by two paintings alluded to in the opening scene, both prefiguring his relationship to Claire—Murillo's "beautiful moon-borne Madonna" (17) and Veronese's *The Marriage at Cana.* Veronese's depiction of the marriage-feast at Cana satisfies Newman's conception, James remarks, "of what a splendid banquet should be" (26). It is, in other words, an opulent vision of worldly desires fulfilled, of aspiration richly realized. Murillo's Madonna, on the other hand, implies the opposite—the impossibility of ideals being fulfilled in this life, and as a consequence the awakening of man's imagination and spiritual life. If the Veronese painting represents the first stage of Newman's relationship to Claire, Murillo's suggests the later one.

Claire is associated through a number of unmistakable touches with Murillo's Madonna, borne off to the moon, withdrawn from this world. Her name Claire means "light," and she seems to Newman to radiate a soft brightness; at Fleurières, before entering the convent, she looks at him with eyes that are like "two rainy autumn moons" (238). Newman is unable to "possess" Claire, yet she becomes part of his inner experience; becomes the standard previously unknown to him by which he may measure the other characters of the novel and himself. Meditating revenge, Newman confronts Mme. d'Outreville and her circle with the evidence against the Bellegardes in his pocket, only to turn away in disgust as he reflects that he would be doing no more than participating in the gossip of an effete clique. Meeting Noémie in Hyde Park not long after this incident, he is able to measure her fully, to see the futility of her life. By the end, Newman puts aside his revenge, his impulse, as he says, to make the Bellegardes feel his "will." In exacting his revenge, he would be acknowledging a personal standard no different from or finer than theirs.

His forswearing his revenge is prepared for by an incident recounted early in the novel, in which, before the Wall Street Exchange, he decides at the last moment not to retaliate against a man who has swindled him. His reasons for turning away are not entirely clear to him, he does not understand them fully himself. Later, however, when the Bellegardes swindle him of Claire, he *knows* why he acts as he does; he has acquired the capacity to discriminate. The incident at the Wall Street Exchange, a monument of worldly values, is full of implication. On his errand of revenge, Newman is driven to the Exchange in a hackney cab that is soiled, "with a greasy line along the top of the drab cushions, as if it had been used for a great many Irish funerals" (34). The cab is even compared to a "hearse" and Newman to a "corpse." By the time he leaves the cab in front of the Exchange, however, he has resolved to let his revenge go, and is at this point depicted in the imagery of rebirth. Relating the incident to Tristram, Newman says: "I seemed to feel a new man inside my old skin, and I longed for a new world" (35). In the new world he seeks in Europe, he passes through the experience of death (Valentin's literally and Claire's in a sense) and "purgatory," and does finally become a "new man." He comes to the threshold of the inner life.

Conclusion

However different *The American* may be formally from *Watch and Ward* and *Roderick Hudson*, it is very much like them in the concerns of its inner plot, since all three deal with achieved or failed transcendence, with narrowed or expanded consciousness. Of the three *The American* has the greatest spontaneity and, in the first half at least, moves furthest out into the world. Yet certain features of the work seem dubious. The Sandian melodrama of the later part trivializes the novel; but, in addition, the book splits apart, being partly a high-spirited comedy and partly a fable of the inner life. Either would have made a novel; united they have a somewhat stitched together effect. Christopher Newman himself is unclearly focused. Supposedly a prototypical Westerner, he has a conscience belonging to New England, and a sense of "fineness" at the end truly Jamesian. And what is one to make of Claire de Cintré? Called an "angel," later said to "fold her wings" (79), she seems an early version of Milly Theale, in *The Wings of the Dove*, who is too good to live. The pressures on Claire from the Bellegardes that force her to withdraw into a convent are not convincingly demonstrated; and partly for this reason her entombment seems a shining if curiously lifeless example to Newman of splendid renunciation.

It is in this earlier part that *The American* seems firm. The comedy of James's American in Paris is a great conception, and much could be written of James's satirical strategies in the first half of the novel. One small incident, however, will suggest its flavor. This incident occurs when Newman tells Madame Bellegarde that he qualifies as Claire's suitor because he is very rich. Old Madame Bellegarde fixes her eyes for a moment on the floor as if gravely offended and perhaps meditating a rebuke, only to look up and ask: "How rich?" (128). In this passage James is solidly on French soil, is in full possession of the old world; he is perfectly at home in the world of manners and forms, and takes obvious relish in observing them. The oddity of *The American* is that it reveals two Jameses at the same time—one temperamentally attuned to social comedy, the other ascetic, morally serious, and distrustful of the world. By the end the exuberance of social comedy, which makes the novel engaging and attractive, is moralized out of existence. *The American* ends in a duet of renunciation that seems *willed* rather than inevitable, and as a result the reader questions the validity of Newman's final, superfine gesture as he stands apart from "all of that," all of life.

Chapter Five

The Europeans:
The Comedy of Cultures

Background

Genesis and Text. James's conquest of London, between 1877 and 1879, provides the context for his short novels of the late 1870s—*The Europeans, Confidence*, and *Washington Square*. In December, 1876, the manuscript of *The American* completed, James returned to London and settled at 3 Bolton Street, which would be home for the next decade. By the spring he became a member of one of London's clubs, and was invited to breakfasts at the home of Richard Monckton Milnes, Lord Houghton—an almost certain indication that he was regarded as a writer on the verge of celebrity. Such celebrity was, in fact, not long in coming. In the winter of 1878, James wrote *Daisy Miller*, the publication of which was something like an international event, making James a widely noticed and discussed writer.

The year 1878 shows James confident of his creative powers and, with evident pleasure, entering into the social life of London. So eagerly was he sought after as a guest at dinners that in the 1878–79 season, he "dined out" 107 times. He came in this way into contact with Browning, Meredith, Arnold, and Pater; with artists such as Whistler and Du Maurier; and with English political figures that included James Bryce and Charles Dilke. His dining out, however, in no way diminished his remarkable capacity for work. By 1879 his productivity had become extraordinary, for in addition to writing *The Europeans, Confidence,* and a number of new stories, he saw through the press a large number of books. In England, in February, he brought out three stories in two volumes (*Daisy Miller,* "An International Episode," and "Four Meetings"); in March, the English edition of *The American;* and in May, a revised edition of *Roderick Hudson.* In August, *Confidence* began its serialization in *Scribner's* magazine; and in October, an English edition of some earlier stories, together with a new one, "The Diary of a Man of Fifty," appeared as *The Madonna of the Future and Other Tales.* In December, his *Hawthorne* brought a triumphant year of publication to a close. Up until *Daisy Miller,* James's books had been published only in America; by the end of 1879, he had "arrived" in London dramatically and all at once.

The Europeans: A Sketch[1] was written immediately after *Daisy Miller.* In a letter of March, 1873, James wrote to Howells agreeing to "squeeze" a new novel that he promised for serialization into one hundred of the *Atlantic's* pages. The novel, as outlined in the letter, would deal with "a mouldering and ascetic old Boston family" visited by one of their kindred from abroad, "a genial, charming youth of a Bohemian pattern," who would convert the New England circle to "epicureanism."[2] Between the time of this sketch and the actual writing of the novel, a number of important changes in its conception occurred; but one feature of *The Europeans* at least, its happy ending, had been settled upon at the beginning and was followed to the letter. As James wrote to his friend Elizabeth Boott, it had been "part of the bargain with Howells" that the novel's "termination should be cheerful and that there should be distinct matrimony."[3]

The Europeans began its serialization in the *Atlantic* in July, 1878, appearing in four monthly installments, and was published in book form by the end of the same year. The critical reception of *The Europeans* was generally unfavorable. Many reviewers were disappointed that it lacked the exuberance of *The American;* and it was frequently said that James's characters were puppets rather than real people.[4] Two reactions to the work are particularly well-known, one that of William James, who wrote to Henry that the novel seemed to him "thin" and "empty." Henry replied, in a conciliatory vein, that he was "aware of its extreme slightness." But he added: "I think you take these things too rigidly and unimaginatively—too much as if an artistic experiment were a piece of conduct, to which one's life were somehow committed."[5]

The criticism of *The Europeans* by Thomas Wentworth Higginson is also frequently cited, since it implies the attitude toward James of New England itself.[6] Higginson's objection was partly that the novel was unhistorical. It showed horse-cars in the streets of Boston a decade before their introduction, and it represented New Englanders themselves as being unsophisticated to an enormously exaggerated degree. James's tone and implied condescension to New England displeased Higginson particularly; and he charged that the novel revealed how "foreign" James was to his native land, and how unable he was either to understand or portray it. Perhaps because of the unfavorable reception *The Europeans* received when it first appeared, James did not include it in the New York Edition. Only since the James revival has the novel come into favor. In his perceptive and influential study of it, Richard Poirier has called *The Europeans* one of James's most brilliant early performances; and F. R. Leavis has characterized it as a small "masterpiece of major quality."[7]

Source and Influence.   *The Europeans* is far different in form and manner from *The American*, yet certain similarities exist. Both are international novels and make use of an intrusion-plot, in which an "outsider" is brought face to face at the end with his or her inability to enter the new world of which they had proposed to take possession. The blank wall of the convent that Newman confronts at the end of *The American* becomes the steep wall of rock that Eugenia is said, finally, to be unable to scale. Both works, too, show a pronounced awareness of the theater. In *The Europeans*, Eugenia has the presence and the arch manner of an actress, and is compared to an actress-in-life; throughout she makes very distinct entrances and exits, and she does so particularly at the beginning

and at the end. The novel moves economically in a series of sharply definite scenes. Many different influences on the dramatic form
of *The Europeans* have been claimed—the graceful and witty com-
edies of Congreve and Marivaux, as well as the "well-made" plays
of Feuillet, Cherbuliez, and Augier. But James's denouement, with
its apparent resolution of difficulties and the giving of many brides
in marriage, suggests a variation on Shakespeare's stage pastorals.

The inspiration for one of the characters of *The Europeans* was
acknowledged by James when he wrote to Elizabeth Boott that
her surmise that Mr. Wentworth was suggested by an actual person
had been correct. "Mr. Wentworth," he wrote to her, "*was* a
reminiscence of Mr. Frank Loring, whose frosty personality I had
in mind in dealing with this figure."[8] Sources for another character,
Eugenia, seem purely literary, and in the background of James's
earlier fiction, two stories are especially relevant. Mrs. Beck in
"Guest's Confession" (1872) anticipates Eugenia, since she, too,
is a coquette who, with worldly motives and an eye toward matrimony, enters into a New England rural scene. "I'll not pretend
I'm not worldly," Mrs. Beck declares, "I'm excessively worldly.
I always make a point of letting people know it." The comedy of
Mrs. Beck is that she is too artificial a person to belong in such a
pastoral setting; and as in the case of Eugenia, she is depicted as
an adventuress in Arcadia. "She might have been fancied," James
writes, "a strayed shepherdess from some rococo Arcadia . . . [but]
Mrs. Beck's morality was not Arcadian; or if it was, it was that of
a shepherdess with a keen eye to the state of the wool and the
mutton market, and a lively perception of the possible advantages
of judicious partnership." In another story, "Four Meetings"
(1877), written just before *The Europeans*, James introduces a
Parisian woman, a bogus countess, into the New England countryside, with comic consequences for her hostess, poor Caroline Spen-
cer. Although Eugenia does not have the same nature as the
"countess," she is like her in being a distinctly European woman
who forms a startling contrast to the other characters. The
"countess" and Mrs. Beck together provide some sort of preparation
at least for Eugenia's sudden appearance in New England.

But Howells's novel "Private Theatricals" (1878) may also have contributed to James's conception of Eugenia and her situation. Before beginning *The Europeans*, James wrote to Howells, saying that he had noted "Private Theatricals" in its *Atlantic* serialization, but planned to postpone reading it until it appeared in book form. He had, however, glanced at it at least, had some idea of its contents; and one cannot help noticing the pronounced similarities that exist between the two novels. Howells's Belle Farrell, like Eugenia, is a coquette, richly endowed with an actresslike nature, who spends a summer in the New England countryside. Out of her natural element at the country house taking seasonal boarders, she has been given a distinctly exotic quality by Howells, who writes of her: "A dim mirage of Oriental fancies rose before Easton, with sterile hills, gleaming lakes, cities, temples of old faith, and priestesses who had the dark eyes, the loose over-shadowing hair, the dusky bloom of Mrs. Farrell." Similarly, James describes Eugenia's "great abundance of . . . dark hair . . . that suggested some Southern or Eastern, some remotely foreign, woman. She had a large collection of ear-rings . . . and they seemed to give a point to her Oriental or exotic aspect" (38–9).[9] Both women, moreover, are pointedly contrasted to their host families, pale, constrained New Englanders—the Woodwards of Howells's novel, the Wentworths of James's. At the end both heroines are, in effect, exiled from the rural settings. Belle Farrell returns to Boston, to act in private theatricals, where her highly styled nature, dissembling, and richly sexual implications may be kept safely from New England life.

The Use of Fairy Tale and Fable

With a foreshortened effect, *The Europeans* begins in Boston, where Eugenia looks out of her hotel room window to a scene below that is a discouraging portent of her arrival in the new world. What she sees is a "dull" spring snow falling over a "narrow grave-yard" (37), beyond which a tall wooden church-spire, painted white, rises high "into the vagueness of the snow-flakes" (38).

In the foreground of this scene pedestrians, as if in flight from the graveyard, scramble aboard a horse-car, James's recurring symbol of democracy. The New England milieu is evoked with a few strokes—its Puritan heritage, its democratic formlessness, its unconsciousness of manners through its habit of high moral abstraction. Eugenia and Felix are ambassadors from a quite different world of elaborately defined manners and forms. Felix is an artist, and Eugenia has affinities with the stage; they represent the "play element" of imagination that is proscribed in New England. The comedy of cultures begins immediately with their first appearance.

Very shortly thereafter, the scene shifts to the countryside not many miles beyond Boston. Supposedly suburban, the setting is actually rural; the Wentworth house has an orchard of apple trees and is set among meadows and fields. It seems to Felix on his arrival that he has never seen anything so "pastoral"; it makes him think of the "golden age" (51), a place of blissful innocence and pleasure in nature that is Arcadian. The Arcadian analogy can be noticed again when Felix reflects that there was "a kind of fresh-looking abundance about it which made him think that people must have lived so in the mythological era, when they spread their tables upon the grass, [and] replenished them from cornucopias" (73). Fragrant with apple trees, it is even compared to paradise. Felix says that he has seen wrongs overseas, but that this "is a paradise" (83). The locality is unnamed, and is so thinly specified that it serves as a ground of morally abstract as well as concretely personal encounter.

Morally abstract encounter is intimated through James's use of fairy tale—the meeting of East and West, and the overcoming of obstacles that can be accounted for only through the operation of wonder. Even in the opening pages, a fabulous meeting between East and West is implied. Entering a Boston street, Felix remarks: "Instead of coming to the West we seem to have gone to the East. The way the sky touches the house-tops is just like Cairo; and the red and blue sign-boards patched over the face of everything remind one of Mahometan decorations" (44). In the next scene, Felix appears at the Wentworth house, where Gertrude is reading a tale in the *Arabian Nights*—that of the Prince Camaralzaman and the Princess Badoura, alluded to earlier in *Watch and Ward*. Camaralzaman and Badoura inhabit opposite parts of the world, yet manage to meet and in one another realize their ideal other self. "At last, looking up," James writes, "[Gertrude] beheld, as it seemed to her, the Prince Camaralzaman standing before her" (51). Near the end, when Gertrude is about to leave with Felix for a life abroad Charlotte asks him what he has *done* to her sister, and he replies: "I think she was asleep; I have waked her up" (148). Camaralzaman's awakening of the sleeping Badoura comes, thus, to incorporate another fairy tale, that of Sleeping Beauty.

But the background of Felix and Eugenia, too, belongs partly to fable. Felix has been a strolling musician and actor in Europe— a romantic background surely, in the tradition of Wilhelm Meister. Eugenia's background belongs to fable perhaps even more strongly. Through her morganatic marriage to the brother of a reigning prince, she is the Baroness Münster, of the principality of Silberstadt-Schreckenstein. The exotic marriage, and the machinations behind the scenes to annul it, make Eugenia's past a "darkly romantic tale" (15). The strangely named Silberstadt-Schreckenstein places Eugenia's past beyond the realm of the familiar or knowable; yet through James's skillful handling and control of tone, it seems actually to exist.

James's Satire of New England

The stylized background of the Europeans is complemented by a stylization in James's treatment of the New Englanders. The New England scene seems almost preposterously sealed off from the rest of the world. With characteristic earnestness, Charlotte declares: "I don't think one should ever try to look pretty" (49), and later she blushes when she is paid a compliment, never having heard anyone's appearance complimented before. The Wentworths have never before heard, and do not know the meaning of, the words "bohemian" and "philistine." Even in respect to their fellow New Englanders, their lives have a vague remoteness. New

England of the late 1840s, as it is pictured in the novel, is notable chiefly for its blankness. Mr. Brand, the Unitarian minister, asks Gertrude if she does not care for "the great questions" (110), and for a moment one seems to hear Margaret Fuller speaking to Waldo Emerson. But apart from one or two allusions to Emerson and the *North American Review*, the age has no dimension and no "life signs." Little wonder that Gertrude's meeting an artist should seem to her the most romantic experience of her life.

In a way that seems appropriate to lives that are highly scrupled but socially unfurnished, the Wentworths have a high, empty parlor. The parlor contains "pale, high-hung engravings" (54), and Mr. Wentworth himself has a "high-featured white face" (59). All of the Wentworths are described as being pale, but Mr. Wentworth's pallor has "semi-mortuary manifestations" (59); and the operation of conscience in him gives him the appearance of "physical faintness" (59). Informed by Felix that he wishes to marry Gertrude, he reacts almost instinctively by asking: "Where are our moral grounds?" (155). In another passage, Felix tells him that he would like to paint him as "an old prelate, an old cardinal," and with his pondering slowness to catch the point of remarks, he exclaims: "A prelate, a cardinal? ... Do you refer to the Roman Catholic priesthood?" (80). Eugenia's morganatic marriage troubles him particularly, and he spends a restless night thinking: "Was it right, was it just, was it acceptable? . . . The strange word 'morganatic' was constantly in his ears; it reminded him of a certain Mrs. Morgan whom he had once known and who had been a bold, unpleasant woman" (60). In his depiction of Mr. Wentworth, James takes liberties with the New England life in the 1840s; Yankee businessmen of that time were neither so unworldly nor so simple as James has depicted Mr. Wentworth. He belongs to the imagination of caricature, to high comedy. His being old and yet, in respect to the world, an infant, is part of the thematic concern in the novel with the contradictions of youth and age—the contradiction particularly that the new world should be hoary with age, while the old world should be gaily young.

Unlike Mr. Wentworth, Felix has an aesthetic rather than moral reaction to life; his last name is Young, and all of his attitudes are youthful. Instead of asking about his "moral grounds," he enquires about the grounds of pleasure; and he finds them everywhere, even in the Puritan capital of Boston. He has the "faculty of enjoyment" (258), and later, very gently, he explains his view of the Wentworths to Gertrude by remarking: "You don't seem to me to get all the pleasure out of life that you might. You don't seem to me to enjoy . . . you take a painful view of life as one may say" (82–83).

Felix and Eugenia Versus the New Englanders

The Europeans, however, deals with more than New England as an environment with, as James says in his *Hawthorne*, "a paucity of ingredients." Its comedy of cultural contrast is intellectual, and in the course of the work it becomes clear that the Europeans are no more perfect than the New Englanders. The visit of the Youngs to their New England relatives contains an element of opportunism; and Eugenia's motives, particularly, are suspect. In the opening scene, she calls herself "ambitious," and it is said that she has come to New England "to make her fortune" (44). Speaking of the Wentworths to Felix before she has yet met them, Eugenia remarks: "Do you suppose if I had not known they were rich I would ever have come?" (43). When she arrives at the Wentworth house, Mr. Wentworth comments that it is natural they should know each other since they are near relatives, and Eugenia replies disingenuously that there comes a moment in life when one reverts irresistibly "to one's natural ties—to one's natural affections" (61). Eugenia tells lies throughout the novel.

Yet Eugenia is not merely a designing woman. The point James makes about her is that she possesses inner complexity. Nothing she says, he writes of her at one point, was "wholly true" but neither was it "wholly untrue" (71). Her less than candid remark about reverting to one's natural affections has just been cited. Yet reading on, one finds Eugenia actually yielding to genuine emotion and natural affection: " 'I came to look—to try—to ask,' she said.

'It seems to me I have done well. I am very tired; I want to rest.'
There were tears in her eyes. The luminous interior, the gentle,
tranquil people, the simple serious life—the sense of these things
pressed upon her with an overmastering force, and she felt herself
yielding to one of the most genuine emotions she had ever known.
'I should like to stay here,' she said. 'Pray take me in'" (65).
Eugenia seeks to manipulate the well-to-do Robert Acton into
marriage, yet later recognizes that she is also in love with him.

In the Wentworth circle, Acton is "the man of the world" (87).
His house is a kind of middle ground between the large square
house of the Wentworths (the windows of which open upon clear,
purifying sunlight) and Eugenia's cottage, which she calls the
"chalet" (the pink silk window blinds of which dim the rooms
and make the play of imagination possible). Acton has been
to China and has brought back a collection of Chinese art objects.
His house, James comments, "had a mixture of the homely and
the liberal, and though it was almost a museum, the large, little-
used rooms were as fresh and clean as a well-kept dairy" (95).
The house suggests that Acton has brought art safely within the
confines of the clean, thin, sunlit air of New England. It implies
an element of susceptibility in him to the imagination, but a need
to keep imagination in its place, to put it in a just New England
perspective. Acton's response to Eugenia, in a similar way, involves an attraction to her held constantly in check by an almost
terrifying need for order.

In a number of telling passages, Acton's hands steal into his
pockets; he is on guard, is described as being "alert" and "vigilant."
Eventually his vigilance becomes a torturously cerebral response to
Eugenia as a kind of puzzle to be solved. "From the first she has
been personally fascinating," James writes, following the train of
Acton's thoughts, "but the fascination now had become intellectual
as well. He was constantly pondering her words and motions, they
were as interesting as the factors in an algebraic problem" (118).
When he permits himself to think of Eugenia as a wife, he
does so in the strange imagery of allowing her into his "citadel,"
opening and then closing the drawbridge, and making her a "toler-

ably patient captive" (118). He sometimes dreams of an illicit relationship with Eugenia, but such a relationship for Acton could occur only at distant Newport or Niagara, not in the precincts of Paradise, where his emotional responses have suffered a crippling paralysis. Near the end, Eugenia makes use of Clifford in an attempt to picque Acton's interest, but her efforts lead to nothing more than his deepened distrust, his belief that he has trapped her into revealing herself unequivocally. His compulsion to bring Eugenia under the containment of his intellect is a kind of violation of Eugenia, since in dispelling the mystery of her personality he is also seeking to do away with her very nature. At the end, Eugenia recognizes that she cannot be acceptable to Acton, and therefore New England, without the loss of her complex identity; and at this point she packs her bag.

The reader's sympathies are sometimes swayed in Eugenia's favor, but it should be remembered that she is not entirely admirable. Even the "dirty-looking lace" (72) with which she decorates her mantel suggests something questionable about her. Despite the charm of her European manners, one can never forget the presence in her of the schemer, and perhaps never more so than at the end when, summing up her mission in New England, she thinks: "Was she to have gained nothing—was she to have gained nothing?" (145). In the Paradise of rural New England, Eugenia may be said to undergo a "fall." Her fall has no allegorical or theological overtones; it is a poetic conceit. She arrives with a great sense of herself, and with the intention of manipulating other people. All of her tastes and many of her expressions are conspicuously foreign (she calls Mr. Wentworth's parlor his "*salon*"), and she seeks to impose these foreign standards on the New Englanders.

Her sense, upon her arrival, that "the good people around her had as regards her remarkable self, no standard of comparison at all gave her a feeling of almost illimitable power" (75). Later, she is disagreeably impressed by Lizzie Acton, who is "positive and explicit almost to pertness," and suggests to her "the possession of a dangerous energy" (95). She has assumed that the American girl, with her directness and lack of nuance, is no match for her. Yet at the end, a version of Lizzie, "a particularly nice young girl" (161), marries Robert Acton, as she fails to do. She discovers that her shadowy nature and accomplished artifice are of no use to her on "the social soil of this big, vague continent" (129). Believing herself at first to have illimitable power, she finds herself at last powerless, and for the first time is compelled to recognize that her European assumptions are not absolutely valid.

The Problematic Ending

The humbling of Madame Münster and the question of how James intends the reader to regard her have divided critics. In *The Comic Sense of Henry James*, Richard Poirier has argued that Eugenia's "banishment" comments most tellingly on New England and its very limited tolerance of social and aesthetic complexity. Eugenia's exclusion, he maintains, implies James's sense of his own relationship to America. In a more recent study, James Tuttleton has disagreed rather pointedly with Poirier, finding *The Europeans* essentially a cultural fable, in which not Eugenia but Felix is the central figure. F. R. Leavis had earlier described *The Europeans* as a dramatic dialectic "in which discriminations for and against are made in respect to both sides, American and European, and from which emerges the suggestion of an ideal positive that is neither." Tuttleton also views *The Europeans* as a dramatic dialectic, but he finds a transcendence of cultural differences implied in Felix. Felix has Eugenia's allegiance to a refinement of life through artifice without her opportunism; and with greater moral sensitivity than Eugenia, he is able to find common ground with the Wentworths. Felix is "gaily idealized," an "allegorical type" in a work that has the quality of fable.

Tuttleton's position is well stated, but one problem with it is that it fails to do justice to Eugenia; she is virtually dismissed as not meriting the reader's esteem, which is surely too narrow and slighting a view of her. More importantly, Felix is not quite the ideal positive Tuttleton claims. It is significant that he is two years under thirty, the age of maturity, and that Eugenia is a few years past thirty. Felix suggests the spirit of joy in life that precedes the creation of art, but he is not fully an artist. He has been a correspondent for an illustrated newspaper; in New England he paints flattering portraits for a hundred dollars apiece; and he admits to Gertrude that he will never be known to the world of art. Although good-natured, he lacks weight, and what is more he lacks focus. He enjoys everything equally, and has no edges. In Europe, he has been a Bohemian, but one so eminently respectable, so free of blemish or excess, that the term loses its meaning. Idealized and allegorical to a degree Felix is, but not to the degree that would enable him to assume the full burden of the novel's theme.

Felix is well matched with Gertrude, whose nature at the beginning is dormant and at the end merely nascent. She has "restless" eyes, but as yet has not given her restless impulses real expression. The most interesting thing about her is not what she is but what she will become in Europe, where the hardness implied in her nature will begin to assert itself and she will acquire "form." It is part of James's impressive control of tone in *The Europeans* that the marriage of Felix and Gertrude, which ostensibly resolves their cultural differences, should be a marriage of juvenescence. Placed in counterpoint to this harmonious resolution is the relationship of Acton and Eugenia, both of mature age, and too formed by their cultures to be able to realize anything more than a stalemate. The marriage of Felix and Gertrude appears to affirm the possibility of transcendence; the failure of the Acton-Eugenia relationship immediately calls such a resolution into question.

The Europeans is a contemplative work of a delicate balance, and there is no animosity toward New England in it on the part of James. Yet it does have complex tones. James's treatment of New England in *The Europeans* contains a degree of affection and tenderness, but it is of somewhat the kind that one finds in his *Hawthorne,* and that leaves no doubt of James's sense of New England as provincial. *The Europeans* has, in any case, and as a fundamental tenet, the incompleteness of the New England point of view; in the sharply focused perspective of manners that James brings to it, New England and its moral reaction look very curious indeed. The hostile review of *The Europeans* by Thomas Wentworth Higginson (ironically, himself a descendant of the Wentworth Puritans of Massachusetts, whose name James's characters have) merely confirms James's point of view. For he disregards the novel's art to reject the work on moral grounds, an irreverence he detects in it toward his native region. Colonel Higginson's review, however, may be contrasted to another reaction to the work by his exact contemporary, James Russell Lowell. After reading *The Europeans* abroad, Lowell wrote to James: "You revived in me the feeling of *cold furniture* which New England has often *goose-fleshed* me with [so] that I laughed and shivered at once."[10] What is striking about *The Europeans* is not, as Higginson claimed, that James did not understand New England and could not represent it, but that he felt it as acutely as he did. Because of the intensity and sharpness of his reaction, the Wentworths spring vividly to life, and open up a new field of portraiture in works that follow. In this brilliant short novel of the most highly finished art, it is not so much Felix as James himself who brings laughter to New England.

Chapter Six

Confidence and *Washington Square* : Intelligence Deceived/ A Parable of the Heart

Confidence

Background: Genesis and Text. *Confidence*[1] was written over a seven-month period, immediately after *The Europeans* and "An International Episode," and ran as a six-part serial in *Scribner's* magazine, from August, 1879, to January, 1880. James received $1,500 for the magazine installments, a substantial figure for a short work; and in February, 1880, the novel was published in book form in America, where it outsold his earlier novels and ran through several editions. Revisions of a minor nature were made from the serial to the book version, in the course of which the twelve chapters of the serial were rearranged into thirty short book chapters. While completing the serial version, James wrote to his family that *Confidence* "will be *very good indeed*—much better than *The Europeans*,"[2] but the critical reception of the novel was generally unfavorable. Reviewers found *Confidence* overly ingenious and implausible, and complained that its characters had been analyzed "to the vanishing point."[3] Even James's old friend Thomas Sergeant Perry, reviewing the novel in the *Atlantic*, asked that James, "with his generous equipment for the task . . . give us novels of a higher flight."[4] James did not include *Confidence* in the New York Edition; and today no serious critical disagreement exists about the work, which is regarded as James's weakest novel.

No definite source for *Confidence* exists, so far as is known; but a number of diverse influences on it have been claimed—the witty and graceful nouvelles of About, Cherbuliez, and Feuillet, as well as the plays of Marivaux, Augier, and Sardou. It has also been suggested that Bernard Longueville, the ratiocinative hero who strenuously analyzes relationships but fails to see the obvious, borrows traits from James's friend Henry Adams.[5] More definitely, *Confidence* has a foreground in James's own story "Osborne's Revenge" (1868), which, like *Confidence*, deals with first impressions that turn out to be erroneous. "Osborne's Revenge" makes use of a paired set of male characters, friends of long-standing but with different temperaments, and a young woman, inscrutable and possibly of a treacherous nature, who enters into their lives. Acting on the assumption that Henrietta Congreve has been the cause of his friend's suicide, Philip Osborne undertakes revenge upon her of a subtle kind, only to fall in love with her and, by the end, to discover that the reality of the matter has been wholly different from his conception of it. Disabused of his illusion finally, he finds that the darkly shaded Miss Congreve is, in reality, the noblest of women.

Background: From Notebook Sketch to Novel.   James's sketch for *Confidence* forms the first entry in his *Notebooks*.[6] In this entry, dated November 7, 1878, the characters of the novel are envisioned as being English, and the central figure is named Harold Stanmer. In an old Italian town, Stanmer meets Bianca (or Blanche) Vane, together with her mother, a perfect lady "of the old English school." Later, he hears from his friend Longueville of his impending marriage to a young woman with whom he is in love but of whom he has a "certain indefinable mistrust." This young lady turns out to be Bianca Vane; and when he is reunited with Longueville, Stanmer agrees to observe her and to offer his disinterested opinion of her character. "I think it may be very interesting here," James notes in the entry, "to mark the degree to which Stanmer—curious, imaginative, speculative, audacious, and yet conscientious, and believing quite in his own fair play—permits himself to experiment upon Bianca—to endeavor to draw her out and make her, if possible, betray herself."

When Longueville returns, Stanmer advises that he believes Bianca is a flirt, and soon after a rupture occurs between Longueville and Bianca. Longueville returns to England where he marries another woman, and later Stanmer again meets Bianca Vane—to discover that he is in love with her, and that his previous impression of her had been mistaken. But when Longueville learns of their engagement, he hurries to join them: to declare that his marriage to the other woman has been a misery to him; to charge Stanmer with having deceived him; and to make a claim on Bianca once more. The notebook entry is consistent with the novel up to this point. The difference that then occurs—and it is a major one—is that in the notebook sketch Longueville's wife dies three days later, with the suspicion left that Longueville "has been the means" of her death. Bianca, in horror, repudiates Longueville, while at the same time breaking with Stanmer. She retires into a religious life, and Stanmer is left to watch over both Bianca and Longueville—and his terrible secret.

The melodramatic ending of the notebook sketch was eliminated in the novel, but almost all of the material leading up to it was retained. The nationality of James's principal characters was altered from English to American, and their names were changed: Stanmer becomes Bernard Longueville, and the original Longueville becomes Gordon Wright; Bianca becomes Angela Vivian, and Gordon's unnamed wife is fleshed out as Blanche Evers. An additional character is invented, Captain Lovelock, a complacent English worldling who acts as escort (and would-be lover) to Blanche in her troubled marriage. At the end there is no violence, no murdered wife. Angela sends Bernard off to London while she and her mother hold therapeutic conversations with Gordon and Blanche, who come gradually to recognize that their inner feelings (their being in love with each other, after all) are at variance with what they have told themselves they feel. As Longueville has been "cured" of his illusion by Angela, so are Gordon and Blanche. An anomaly among James's novels after *Watch and Ward*, *Confidence* has an unambiguously happy ending.

   The Weakness of Confidence.   The happy ending, however, the concluding section in which Angela becomes "a ministering angel" (197),[7] seems quite unreal. Her inscrutable smile at the beginning becomes a coy smirk as she reflects, in effect, "what fools men are!" A figure of shadow and mystery in Italy, she becomes by the end as clear as daylight, virtually another character. Angela's mother undergoes a similar transformation from apparent complexity to indubitable simplicity. In Baden-Baden, Mrs. Vivian is depicted as "a Puritan grown worldly—a Bostonian relaxed" (56), and one expects to see the unfolding of a complex nature; but at the end she is merely full of gentleness and consideration. The provocative sketching of mother and daughter in the opening section seems by the end merely a trick of presentation.

   Blanche Evers and Captain Lovelock, however, have no sharply personal identity at any time. Blanche is described early in the novel as a version of "the American pretty girl" (26), but she has no affinity whatever with Daisy Miller or Bessie Alden, whom James had just created. She is a chatterbox and that is all, as dimensionless and stereotyped a figure as Captain Lovelock, the improvident roué; and they exist in the novel essentially as foils. Lame, too, is the characterization of Gordon Wright, who behaves as if he has no common sense. Why, for example, is he so slow to see that he loves his wife? Why, over a matter that was ended years before, would he act as he does, charging his friend with treachery and making an impassioned claim upon Angela? He seems to exist merely to advance James's plot.

   That the elaborate working out of the plot has been given priority over other considerations normally paramount with James can be seen in other ways as well. *Confidence* begins in Siena, and later moves to Baden-Baden, London, New York, and Paris; but in no instance are these settings integrated appreciably with what happens there. As setting and background they are not filled in, and their vagueness adds to the sense one has that the novel takes place in a void. That both Bernard and Gordon are rich and idle, do not work, and are likely to travel to distant parts of the world at a moment's notice, gives them the quality of shadow figures existing in a limbo of purely personal "relationships." The thinness or insubstantiality of these relationships is illustrated by Gordon. Supposedly too logical in his way of thinking, he seems, quite the opposite, a man incapable of any kind of sustained thought; and it is difficult to take any passionate interest in him or in whether or not he is reconciled to Blanche or to Angela. The happy life to which Gordon and Blanche go off at the end is a comment on the daydream quality of the novel, in which a serious interest in character is sacrificed to symmetry and design, schematization and idea.

The Relevant Theme—the "Experimenter" Baffled.   If *Confidence* were regarded purely on the level of its narrative movement, it would have to be considered a work of remarkable grace. It is a pleasure to read and dramatic to an unusual degree, brief scene following swiftly upon brief scene, frequently with striking effect. Certain of its incidents and recognitions are rendered magically. Particularly effective is the sequence beginning with Bernard's return to France, where, from the window of his room at Havre, he looks out upon a dirty yellow wall, a "blank wall, which struck him in some degree as a symbol of his own moral prospect" (121). Acting purely on impulse, he journeys into the countryside, where he stops at the small, out-of-the-way resort of Blanquais-les-Galets. There, sleeping on the beach, he has a dream in which he seems to see a young woman before him, and then wakes to see Angela, and to make a recognition that fills him "with a kind of awe" (135)—that he is, has been, in love with her.

But the real interest of *Confidence* is in what it shows of James's evolving thematic concerns during the period of the late 1870s. A line of development exists, for example, from Winterbourne and Robert Acton to Bernard Longueville. Winterbourne attempts to fix Daisy Miller to a formula, and Acton comes to regard Eugenia as an algebraic problem that he would find it fascinating to solve, and he consequently plays a kind of "game" with her, attempting to find the right formula for her. In *Confidence*, James's conception of a young man who attempts, with nearly mathematical precision, to entrap a girl into revealing herself becomes a central concern. At Baden-Baden, Mrs. Vivian is seen perusing a book by the French philosopher Victor Cousin, an allusion that quietly calls attention to Cousin's doctrine of the reasoning faculty's ability directly to perceive the absolute. Cousin's notion of the sufficiency of mind or reason to account for life is what the novel proceeds to test. Both Bernard and Gordon are described as committed "reasoners," and are specifically associated with scientific experimentation. Gordon has settled in Germany, "the land of laboratories" (20), where he pays the expenses of "difficult experiments" (20); the word "experiment" appears as often in the the novel as its counterword "confidence."

Early in the novel Bernard Longueville is portrayed not only as Gordon's friend but also as his critic. He reflects at the beginning that "nothing could better express [Gordon's] attachment to the process of reasoning things out than [his] proposal that [he] should come and make a chemical analysis—a geometrical survey— of the lady of his love" (19). As Bernard goes to Germany to meet him, he thinks: "Gordon's mind . . . has no atmosphere; his intellectual process goes on in the void. There are no currents or eddies to affect it. . . . His premises are neatly arranged, and his conclusions are perfectly calculable" (20). As the novel proceeds, however, it becomes apparent that Bernard and Gordon are not the temperament opposites they at first seem but actually counterparts of one another. Bernard himself, a man "of a contemplative and speculative turn" (76), has a similar reliance upon deductive reasoning. He is called an "observer," and the idea of making the girl "a subject of speculative scrutiny" (79) creates in him a sense of "intellectual excitement" (76).

In Baden-Baden, Bernard enjoys the "game" of finding Angela out: "it became a kind of entertaining suspense to see how long she would keep [her secret]" (39). But Bernard turns out to be the dupe of his own perceptions. Angela understands his intentions immediately, and later she remarks to him: "Did it ever strike you that my position at Baden was a charming one—knowing that I had been handed over to you to be put under a microscope—like an insect with a pin stuck through it" (154). Moreover, he has been so blinded by his ratiocinative procedures that he does not grasp that his "excitement" is actually due to his being in love with Angela. Bernard's enlightenment comes only in the course of time, as he gradually discovers the powerlessness of his own reason and will. At the gambling tables of Baden-Baden, he is disturbed to find that he wins a large sum unaccountably, through no exertion of his intelligence but merely through blind chance; and blind chance sends him to Blanquais-les-Galets, where his dream consciousness becomes a daylight recognition. What he recognizes by the end is that the mystery of love and emotional growth is impenetrable by reason or logic. The ending of *Confidence* is genial, as genial as a classic comedy of errors; but buried in the novel is a serious theme not as yet fully explored—that of the "experimenter" who violates the "heart" of a young woman. It is in this respect that *Confidence* leads directly into *Washington Square*. The experimenter's "intellectual excitement" that becomes a form of "entertainment" for Bernard Longueville is seen next in Dr. Sloper, but it is handled altogether more seriously. Even in as weak a work as *Confidence* there is something that can be salvaged, for in *Washington Square* James writes one of the most masterful short novels of his career.

Washington Square

Background: Genesis and Text. *Washington Square*[8] was begun immediately after *Confidence* and *Hawthorne*, while James was visiting on the Continent. Intended originally as a short story for the *Atlantic*, it expanded to the length of a short novel. It was published in serial form simultaneously in England, in the *Cornhill Magazine* (June–November, 1880), and in America, in *Harper's* (July–December, 1880). With virtually no revision, it was published in book form early in 1881 in both countries. James's own comments on *Washington Square* in letters are puzzlingly harsh and difficult to account for. To Howells, he characterizes it as "a poorish story . . . the writing of which made me feel acutely the want of . . . 'paraphernalia' ";[9] and to Grace Norton, he describes it as "a slender tale of rather too narrow an interest."[10] To his brother William, who liked *Washington Square*, he comments that the "only good thing in the story is the girl."[11] James appears to have held a slighting opinion of the work throughout his life. In 1907, while he was preparing the New York Edition, he wrote to Robert Herrick: "I have tried to read over *Washington Square* and I can't, and I fear it must go!"[12] *Washington Square* was not included in the New York Edition.

Reviews of *Washington Square* in America were generally unfavorable.[13] The reviewer for the *Dial* described James as "beyond doubt the cleverest writer who now entertains the public with fiction," but dismissed *Washington Square* as a waste of his talent.[14] Horace Scudder, writing in the *Atlantic*, found the novel's characters "elaborate nonentities," and complained that James's mocking wit allowed the heroine not even pity or sympathy. Repeatedly the words "clever" and "superficial" were used to characterize both James and the novel. The critic for the *Literary World* saw little or no worth in this "clever bit of psychological anatomy, . . . [this] piece of literary dilettantism."[15] The reviewer for the *Independent* remarked that *Washington Square* "is the work of a supremely clever literary artisan, self-conscious, artificial in every sense of the word, and thoroughly un-American."[16] Many of the reviews complained that *Washington Square* lacked local color, and failed to produce adequately either the period in which it was set or the society about which it was written.

In later criticism, and in a way that recalls its original reviews, *Washington Square* has been faulted for its failure to fill in its social setting. C. Hartley Grattan, writing in 1932, maintained that the novel in no way required its New York scene. Lacking any depth of commitment to local realism, he wrote, James was "well advised to abandon this field to William Dean Howells."[17] More recently, J. I. M. Stewart has found in *Washington Square* not only no social background but no deep level of artistic excitement. The novel, he remarks, "is neither rich nor promising. Its people are alive, but life does not pulse in it or them."[18] But even in the earlier criticism, one notices a recognition of *Washington Square* by some as a remarkable work. Rebecca West, in her short book on James in 1916, calls *Washington Square* "James's first important work, . . . a work of great genius."[19] In more recent times, Morton Zabel argues that *Washington Square,* in its "concise perfection," initiates James's middle period, in which he established his mastery, essential subject, style, and relationship to his age.[20] To F. R. Leavis, *Washington Square* is one of James's great achievements in the short novel form. The stature of *Washington Square* today is high indeed, and it is commonly called a masterpiece. In his recent study of James in relation to the Victorians, Donald David Stone remarks that "*Washington Square* is not only James's best work of the 1870's but one of the great late Victorian novels."[21]

Background: Source and Influence.   The immediate source for *Washingston Square* is recorded in James's *Notebooks,* under the date of February 21, 1879.[22] In the entry, James relates the account told to him the evening before by his friend Mrs. Kemble, the celebrated actress, of her younger brother's engagement many years before to a "dull, plain, common-place girl" who stood to inherit a fortune from her father. Young Kemble was a handsome ensign in a marching regiment; selfish and "luxurious," he was interested in the girl only for her money. The girl's father (the master of King's College, Cambridge—"the old Doctor") disapproved of the engagement and threatened to disinherit his daughter if she should marry Kemble. Convinced that the father meant to keep his word, Kemble jilted her. Later the father died, and the girl came into her inheritance. Perhaps ten years after the engagement, Kemble returned to England from knocking about in the world (still a "handsome, selfish, impecunious soldier") and once again sought to pay his addresses to her.

She turned him away, even though she cared for no other man. "H. K.'s selfishness had overreached itself and this was the retribution of time."

In adapting the story for fiction, James gave his characters an American nationality and placed them in an American setting familiar to him from his youth; but many essentials of the account are preserved in the relationship of Catherine and Morris—the threatened disinheritance, following which Morris disengages himself from Catherine; his absence for years, and attempt to ingratiate himself with her again after her father's death; her turning him away although she cares for no one else. Even Mrs. Kemble's advice to the girl that if she married her brother without her inheritance he would take out the spite of his disappointment on her is incorporated into the novel, in Dr. Sloper's forecast to Catherine of Morris's likely conduct. The account contains, too, a reference to another sister who attempts to bring Kemble and the girl together at this later time, a reference that may have inspired the character and the confidante role of Mrs. Penniman.

In shaping *Washington Square* from the raw material of his notebook entry, however, James was affected by literary sources. Balzac's *Eugénie Grandet* (1833) seems important to the work conceptually. A work James admired and knew well, *Eugénie Grandet* deals with a young heroine and a situation similar in many respects to the heroine and situation of *Washington Square*. Both works are of approximately the same length, and are set back in time to a "simpler" era. *Eugénie Grandet* is a "study" of provincial life; and *Washington Square* is a "study" of provincial New York a generation before the Civil War. In both cases, milieu plays a part, since it restricts the heroines's opportunities for experience. Balzac's provincial setting is a narrowly patriarchal environment in which men have the active or dominant role, and in which women's opportunities for enlargement are confined to love and marriage, other means of expression being closed to them. For a woman to be blighted in love and marriage is to be blighted tragically; and it is exactly such a fate that Eugenie is made to endure. *Eugénie Grandet* is the story of a young woman who undergoes a lonely suffering and is, in effect, martyred by her world. Its correspondences to *Washington Square* are quite remarkable.

Eugénie and Catherine are both "heiresses," and when the novels open are approximately the same age—in their early twenties. They are not beautiful, but have inner goodness and purity of emotion; naive and trusting, they have had sheltered upbringings and know little of the world. Into their quiet lives, ruled over by a father with a psychological fixation, enters a handsome young man who, before long, pledges his love. The girls are torn between their obedience to their father, whose word is law, and their fidelity to the lover, in whom they place an absolute trust—only in the end to be deceived and jilted by him. In Balzac's novel, the father and lover are markedly different from one another as characters, and yet are alike in their self-centeredness and worldly values. They come to represent the worldliness to which the naive and generous Eugénie is victimized. At the end, after her father's death, Eugénie lives on, with the stiff habits of an old maid, in her father's house. "Such," Balzac concludes, "is the life story of this woman who is not of this world, though living in it, who born to be a magnificent wife and mother, has neither husband, children, nor family." In *Washington Square*, Catherine's life, the suffering inflicted upon her by her father and lover, has distinct parallels with Eugénie's; and she, too, is alone at the end in a house of memories. The houses, in fact, frame the heroines's experience, since almost all of the action takes place in them, and they become, finally, symbolic of the heroines's losses, constricted lives, and exclusion from life.

Yet in *Washington Square* James introduced refinements of conception of which Balzac was incapable; and the relationship of Dr. Sloper and his daughter, particularly, reveals another influence—that of Hawthorne. Immediately before composing *Washington Square*, James wrote his critical biography of Hawthorne, immersing himself once again in his fiction; and it is not entirely surprising, therefore, that Hawthorne's influence on James should reappear at this time. In *The American Scene* (1907), James compared his homeland, after an absence of many years, to "a huge Rappaccini garden, rank with each variety of the poison-plant of the money-passion."[23] This allusion to Hawthorne's "Rappaccini's Daughter" is one of a number in James's writing; James regarded the story as one of Hawthorne's supreme tales, and he incorporated it into the conception of certain stories of his own, such as "Eugene Pickering" (1874) and "Benvolio" (1875). As in *Washington Square*, "Rappaccini's Daughter" involves a set of three characters in a triangular relationship—domineering father, pure and meek daughter, and prospective lover. In it, Dr. Rappaccini is a scientist overweeningly proud of intellect who, for the sake of a psychological experiment, sacrifices his daughter's life. In *Washington Square*, Dr. Sloper has strong affinities with Dr. Rappaccini, for he, too, has a pure and meek daughter under his trust and guardianship, whose life he sacrifices for the sake of an intellectually gratifying experiment. Dr. Sloper is even called a "scholarly doctor" (162)[24] and he comes to stand for intellectual pride as much as his daughter represents purity of heart. In *Confidence*, James explores the idea of characters who "experiment" upon the "heart" of a girl; and in this way he begins to approach his conception of *Washington Square*. By the time of *Washington Square*, however, James's conception has been sharpened by Hawthorne's conception of Dr. Rappaccini, whose violation of his submissive and trusting daughter's soul becomes the archetypal model for James's envisioning of Dr. Sloper's violation of Catherine. Although a novel of unsparing realism, *Washington Square* is informed, at its core, by Hawthorne's conception of the Unpardonable Sin.[25]

Dr. Sloper and Morris Townsend as Character Doubles.
The house on Washington Square dominates the action of the novel, but it is not the first house mentioned in the work that Dr. Sloper inhabits. Several years before Catherine's twenty-first birthday, he had moved uptown from a house "of red brick, with granite copings and an enormous fanlight over the door" (170) at the older, lower end of Manhattan Island. The neighborhood had by then become "commercialized," and Dr. Sloper looked for a quieter address. "The ideal of quiet and genteel retirement, in 1835," James remarks, "was found in Washington Square, where the Doctor built himself a handsome, modern, wide-fronted house,

with a big balcony before the drawing-room windows, and a flight of marble steps ascending to a portal which was also faced with white marble. This structure, and many of its neighbours, which it exactly resembled, were supposed, forty years ago, to embody the last results of architectural science" (171). The house is clearly related to Dr. Sloper's sense of himself; it is distinctly "solid," as the doctor thinks of himself as being. Dr. Sloper knows what his "place" is in the social hierarchy of New York, and the house reflects this assumption.

To Morris Townsend, the house on Washington Square represents his own aspirations. His last name, which could be written "town's end," underscores his position as an outsider. He is without a house, living with or upon his sister, Mrs. Montgomery, who has a humble house of an indeterminate address somewhere in the dim distances of Second Avenue. Morris's attraction to the Sloper house is immediate and profound. When he dines there fairly early in the work, he reflects with satisfaction on the completeness and good taste of Dr. Sloper's wine cellar. Later, when Catherine and her father go abroad, Morris calls on Mrs. Penniman and makes himself at home in the doctor's study, smoking a leisurely cigar in the same chair in which Dr. Sloper had smoked his. This act of usurpation is not witnessed by the doctor, but it is imagined by him while he is in Europe. Proprietor and pretender to the house, the two men are locked in conflict throughout the novel. It is in terms of the house that Morris at times regards his courtship of Catherine, as can be noticed in the scene where he returns to Washington Square with Mrs. Penniman after a discussion with her of his most advantageous next move. "His eyes," James writes, "travelled over it. . . . He thought it a devilish comfortable house" (224).

In their will to dominate, both men regard Catherine as they might "property" that is in contention, and the antagonism between them is particularly strong because they are in many ways similar. Dr. Sloper has been a successful man, and knows it; but Morris, too, is worldly, and is alert to ways in which to advance himself. Even in their personal backgrounds, similarities can be noticed. Dr. Sloper came from modest circumstances and married an heiress. He married her, as James says, "for love," and managed a successful career that was in every way honest. One man has married an heiress, the other wishes to, and between them there is great opposition; it is as if the doctor, for all his probity, recognizes an assaultive or aggressive impulse in Morris that he understands personally only too well.

Dr. Sloper and Morris are linked in other ways as well, since certain of the doctor's characteristics can be seen in the younger man. One of his most conspicuous traits, for example, is his irony; and Morris, too, possesses an ironical attitude, as can be seen when he courts Catherine with "a smile of respectful devotion in his handsome eyes" (182). Dr. Sloper and Morris are both said to be "clever," and more than once Dr. Sloper, of an intellectual nature himself, insists that Morris is intelligent. "I can see by your physiognomy," the doctor tells him, "that you are extremely intelligent" (195); and later he describes him to Catherine as a young man "who is, indeed, very intelligent" (203). Moreover, these two men, associated with intellect, sometimes think in the imagery of mathematics and science. Dr. Sloper explains to Mrs. Penniman that he has taken the measure of Catherine and Morris, and shall not relent in his opposition to their marriage, since a "geometrical proposition" does not relent; and Morris, in turn, sees the doctor's opposition as an unknown quantity in a mathematical problem that must be solved. The importance of these intellectual gentlemen in Catherine's life is summed up by James's remark near the end that from "her own point of view the great facts of her career were that Morris Townsend had trifled with her affection, and that her father had broken its spring" (234).

One weakness in James's conception of Morris is that he is a character without complexity. As he first appears, his nature is not fully clear, although it is suspect; but at the end of chapter twenty-five, he is presented rather abruptly as a conceited and wholly unsympathetic fortune-hunter. His conduct thereafter is predictable, since it derives partly from the fortune-hunter of stage and fiction. Dr. Sloper is elaborated more fully and is a more distinctive conception, but in at least one respect he is puzzling, since an element of his nature seems not to have been filled in. His attitude toward women is, as James says, "not exalted" (165); indeed, he seems to regard the "imperfect sex" (166) with barely concealed distaste. For this reason his having been in love with and ideally married to the late Catherine Harrington seems somewhat hypothetical. Women do not "stir" Dr. Sloper, and it is difficult to believe that they once had. Men, however, do not "stir" him either. One can picture him best in his sexually asceptic study. A modern novelist, aware of Freud, would have made some effort to account for Dr. Sloper's misogny, have located the sexual block or frustration behind his bitterness. James accounts for the sense of frustration in him through the premature death of his wife in childbirth, for which he holds Catherine responsible; but this explanation would have more weight if one could believe that Dr. Sloper had been capable of loving a woman. One feels that he responds to Catherine as he does, and "such as she was" (164), not only because she is plain but also, embitteringly, because she is female; and as a result the reader is left with a sense of unexplained currents in his psychology.

Yet even with this blank space in his nature, Dr. Sloper is a great character. He is one of the characters in James's fiction that one always remembers, and he is felt in the great way, with a sharp effect on one's nerves. The whole nature of his relationship to Catherine is crystallized in the scene where Catherine tells him of her engagement to Morris. "And as she pronounced her lover's name," James remarks, "Catherine looked at him. What she saw was her father's still grey eye and his clear-cut definite smile. She contemplated these objects for a moment, and then she looked back at the fire; it was much warmer" (201). He habitually addresses his child with an irony that wounds, that is intended to diminish her dignity and self-respect. His irony is a form of aggression upon her small and uncertain identity, and even Catherine, slow thinking as she is, comes to understand what his irony implies.

Late in the work she tells Morris that they must expect nothing from her father for a reason stronger even than his disapproval of him. He is, she explains, "not very fond of me" (258).

More than that, Catherine's own loving nature becomes the source of an amusing diversion for Dr. Sloper, an opportunity to exercise his wits. Virtually in the vocabulary of a chemical experiment, he estimates Catherine's reactions under stress, and the consequences that would follow from them. Chillingly, what he relies upon in these calculations is her gentle trust in him. In a focal scene, he tells her that if she sees Morris again, she will cause him the greatest grief of his life. Then, leaving the room and standing by the closed door, he listens, hearing no sound but knowing that Catherine stands stricken on the other side; and it suddenly comes over him that she will "stick." Her "sticking" strikes him as mirthful, as offering "a prospect of entertainment" (231). In this scene, Dr. Sloper has almost the quality of a monster, a man so self-centered that he cannot feel for others.

In this respect, he is, again, like Morris. Dr. Sloper "plays" with Catherine's emotions, and so does Morris. Both calculate their moves and "game plays." Both possess skill and cunning, but are deficient in pity. In a finely rendered moment that comments on Dr. Sloper tellingly, James remarks that the loss of Dr. Sloper's wife and infant son might have been a doubtful recommendation of him as a physician but that New York society *"pitied him too much to be ironical"* (164; my italics). What the ironical doctor resents most deeply in Morris is his cool assumption of his importance over others, objects made conveniently to serve his will. At several points, he charges that Morris is "selfish," and it is on this basis that he objects to him as a son-in-law. But what he sees in Morris is present as fully in himelf—his self-importance, and habit of regarding others as objects. Were Catherine to marry Morris, he would, in fact, be egotistical and selfish, and have no real respect for her. But would her position in that case be different from her present one with her father, whose egotism and lack of respect for her are glaring?

Mrs. Penniman.   The doctor's sister, Mrs. Penniman, is also self-centered; and her self-centeredness blinds her to Catherine's suffering. She betrays her trust, as her guardian, from the beginning, inviting the attentions of a young man she ought, had she any sense, to have discouraged. She urges Morris's suit insistently, and is an ever-present reminder of him within the Sloper house. Through Catherine, in fact, she indulges in a vicarious love affair with Morris, sends him letters secretly, and holds trysts with him. During the absence abroad of Dr. Sloper and Catherine, she encourages him to make himself at home in the house; and in a wonderful line, she remarks that "I may almost say that *I* have lived with him" (252). Her florid and sentimental imagination prevents her from perceiving the human consequences of her actions.

Mrs. Penniman's encouragement of Morris is an indulgence of her own pleasure at Catherine's expense. Furthermore, she makes comparisons, and on the deepest level is Morris's partisan rather than her niece's. At one point she even instructs Morris that he may back out of the engagement. "You may postpone—you may change about; she won't think the worse of you" (240), she tells him; and in this way she becomes another of Catherine's manipulators. "In the first place," Mrs. Penniman reflects, "Morris *must* get the money, and she would help him to it. . . . If Morris had been her son, she would certainly have sacrificed Catherine to a superior conception of his future; and to be ready to do so, as the case stood, was therefore even a finer degree of devotion. Nevertheless, it checked her breath a little to have the sacrificial knife, as it were, suddenly thrust into her hand" (269). It is Catherine's fate to be "sacrificed" by all three of the people in whom she places her trust. In his study of James's imagery, Robert Gale has observed that fully a tenth of the images in *Washington Square* deal with warfare or weapons.[26] Sharp, murderous knives are particularly prominent in the work, as those who encircle Catherine deliver stab after stab.

The Portrait of Catherine.   It is in comparison with her tormentors, however, that Catherine achieves the dignity she does. It has been mentioned that although Dr. Sloper is without pity, those who know him, following the death of his wife and child, feel too much pity for him to be ironical about his practice. But Catherine, too, has a compassion the doctor lacks. Deeply wounded herself, she yet feels for *him*. "She pitied him," James comments, "for the sorrow she had brought upon him" (242). At other points in the novel Catherine's remarkable selflessness is shown; and there is a poignant passage in which, many years later, she rereads the letter Morris had sent to her, breaking off their engagement. "The letter," James remarks, "was beautifully written, and Catherine, who kept it for many years after this, was able, when her sense of the bitterness of its meaning and the hollowness of its tone had grown less acute, to admire its grace of expression" (279).

It is by comparison with Mrs. Penniman, too, that Catherine gains in stature. Mrs. Penniman falsifies everything she feels. She would have Catherine go to Morris's residence and indulge in tears and reproaches, "an image so agreeable to Mrs. Penniman's mind that she felt a sort of aesthetic disappointment at its lacking, in this case, the harmonious accompaniment of darkness and storm" (274). Mrs. Penniman's imagination belongs to romantic melo-drama, in which emotions are exaggerated, made histrionic, and cheapened. She cannot understand Catherine's refusal to drama-tize her suffering. In the later part of *Washington Square*, James refers to "the grief that does not speak" (275), an allusion to *Macbeth*, in the scene where Macduff is informed that his wife and all his children have been cruelly murdered. Catherine, at this point, has lost everyone she has loved and held dear; but her grief is too great for public show, too sacred to be cheapened or used in an effort to manipulate others. Her stubbornly silent suffer-ing is the poetry of authenticity.

With her dull, gentle eyes and awkward shyness, Catherine makes an unlikely heroine. She is called "poor Catherine" not only by Dr. Sloper but also by James himself, and it would be easy to take a condescending view of her. Mrs. Penniman remarks that "nothing could be simpler than Catherine" (238); Morris, when his inner thoughts are suddenly revealed, thinks of her as "a young woman of inferior characteristics" (219); and Dr. Sloper everywhere disparages her, calling her "ugly" when she is merely plain. It seems to him "a grievous pity that his only child was a simpleton" (190). At other points he reflects that Catherine "isn't romantic" (167) or a woman "of great spirit" (216).

But it should be noted that, however unerringly he has measured Morris, Dr. Sloper is repeatedly mistaken about his daughter. As for her being, as he claims, "inanimate," or without inner spirit or life, the red satin dress she wears (more than once and sometimes by a glowing fireplace) implies a great deal of inarticulate emotion, or susceptibility to feeling in her. Her taste for romantic opera music, particularly that of Bellini and Donizetti, carries the same implication. It is her ability to feel that distinguishes her from the emotionally artificial Mrs. Penniman, and from Dr. Sloper and Morris. Nor is Catherine a simpleton. Her intelligence is decidedly not quick, but she does come to make recognitions. After the engagement party at Mrs. Almond's, Catherine gives evasive answers for the first time to her father, saying that she thought "nothing particular" of the young man to whom she had been speaking, and did not remember his name. These small dissimulations mark the first stage of her independence from her father, and of her developing awareness.

Later, in the conflict of choices forced upon her, she makes an important discovery that is like her birth into independent existence:

Catherine meanwhile had made a discovery of a very different sort; it had become vivid to her that there was a great excitement in trying to be a good daughter. She had an entirely new feeling, which may be described as a stage of expectant suspense about her own actions. She watched herself as she would have watched another person, and wondered what she would do. It was as if this other person, who was both herself and not herself, had suddenly sprung into being, inspiring her with a natural curiosity as to the performance of untested functions. (216)

This moment shows her growth into awareness, into a life created from moral choices. By the end, she comes to recognize the falsity of Mrs. Penniman, the hollowness of Morris, and the lack of feeling for her of her father. She acquires more awareness than the other characters had presumed her capable; but, even more importantly, and against the greatest odds, she establishes her own identity.

The other characters have presumed her inanimate and able to be bent to their wills. Mrs. Penniman describes her as a type who "clings" to others; and Dr. Sloper reflects that "poor Catherine was not defiant; she had no genius for bravado" (194). But she has defiance of a kind that they cannot understand, a tenacious will to be "good." Her tenacity is at first underestimated. When Dr. Sloper finds amusement in the idea that she will "stick," he does not realize what her "sticking" will mean. He remarks that she "will do as I have bidden her" (216), but, in fact, as the novel progresses, he loses his power over her. In the scene abroad, set in the Alps, he attempts to frighten her into submission, with the threat of abandoning her to a life as lonely and desolate as the ravine before which they stand. Her courage in refusing to submit to his coercion at this point is the more impressive because she knows that such a prospect of desolate loneliness is real.

Unable to force his will upon her, and thus deny her an identity of her own, Dr. Sloper lives with a sense of increasing frustration, and is finally no longer sure he understands the daughter he had once confidently fitted to "type." He describes himself as having passed "into the exasperated stage" (261), and at the end his reduction of her inheritance to a fraction of what it had been, accompanied by an ugly disparagement of her in the codicil of the will as a woman interested in "unscrupulous adventurers" (287), reveals the loss of his irony and self-control. He becomes the victim of his own victimization of another. Thwarted, too, at the end is Morris, whose exploitative calculations have brought him none of the things he has coveted. When he returns, at the age of forty-five (fat, bald, and unsuccessful), to the house on Washington Square, and attempts to make up to Catherine, she is unresponsive. He leaves the house with as much incomprehension of her as Dr.

Sloper, and is last seen in his baffled frustration and powerlessness exclaiming "Damnation!"

The House at the End. In the ending of *Washington Square*, as throughout the work, the house has an integral relation to the drama enacted within it. Local background does not enter elaborately into the novel, and its absence deprives it of a kind of richness it might otherwise have had. But it is specified enough to be meaningful. Early in the work attention is called to the northward movement of the city. Arthur Townsend, Morris's cousin who marries Mrs. Almond's daughter and works in a brokerage house, speaks of his buying a house uptown, and then moving further uptown every few years, with the rapid expansion northward. Arthur Townsend is not filled in as a character, he is merely a type. But although sketched only briefly, it is clear that he is superficial. He compares his moving ever "higher" in the city to Longfellow's "Excelsior," and makes a somewhat sharp remark about Morris's wanting to know all the pretty young ladies—"like Mrs. Penniman!" (179), while he laughs inwardly. Arthur Townsend is not deeply feeling and his migration ever further upward in the city, while Washington Square is left behind as a small pocket of the past, suggests the difference between his life and Catherine's. Catherine has the name of a martyred saint, St. Catherine, and the house on Washington Square embodies the martyrdom of her innocence. James intimates at one point that she will live to a great age; she will perhaps live on to a greater age even than Miss Bordereau in "The Aspern Papers," always enclosed in the memories that will exclude her from "life."

Yet the house suggests more than her suffering. It implies the difference between time and change, and what is fixed and unchanging; between surface and depth; between the externally lived life and the life that is lived inwardly. Mrs. Penniman perceives Catherine as being weak-willed, but it is *she* who is without will, who truckles to Morris, and by comparison one is conscious of Catherine's firmness and integrity. She is unaggressively stubborn, her prayers are purged of all violence, but she has character and

even force. It might even be said that her life in the house on
Washington Square is not wholly one of desolation. The fancy
work she does may give her the stiff quality of a spinster, one at
whom an Arthur Townsend would be inclined to laugh. But her
small yet rich needlework is faintly reminiscent of Hester Prynne's
in *The Scarlet Letter*; it suggests a life gone "underground," lived
inwardly.

In this respect, one recalls the moving scene at the end where
Catherine meets Morris again after many years, and compares the
bare, soiled reality of Morris with the richness of her inner life
that her love for him has nourished. "She continued to look at
him," James writes, ". . . and as she did so she made the strangest
observation. It seemed to be he, and yet not he; it was the man
who had been everything, and yet this person was nothing. How
long ago it was—how old she had grown—*how much she had lived*!
She had lived on something that was connected with *him*, and she
had consumed it in doing so" (293; my italics). The word "faith"
is used several times in regard to Catherine, and she is the novel's
believer, who adheres to the purity of feeling, in which the world
cannot believe and would only corrupt. She pays a fearful price for
her virtues. But she, at least, represents something positive. Dr.
Sloper and Morris gain nothing from their "use" of Catherine, who
refuses to use them; and Mrs. Penniman receives neither gratitude
nor respect from Morris for aiding him in his attempt to advance
himself through her niece. The "more she professed her willingness to serve him," James observes, "the greater fool [Morris]
thought her" (265). Dr. Sloper, Morris, and Mrs. Penniman all
violate Catherine's "heart," but it is "heart" not "head" that James
commemorates in *Washington Square*. Catherine alone at the end
has been given a mysteriously indefinable breadth of existence as
she persists in her stubborn survival, through the power of simple
goodness.

Chapter Seven

The Portrait of a Lady: The Caging of the Beautiful Striver

Background

Genesis and Text.   An entry in James's notebooks indicates that when he began work on *The Portrait of a Lady*[1] in Florence, early in 1880, he was returning to a fragmentary beginning written some time earlier. "At the Hotel de l'Arno, in a room in that deep recess, in the front," he recorded, "I began *The Portrait of a Lady*— that is, I took up, and worked over, an old beginning, made long before."[2] Exactly when this "old beginning" was written is not known, but a reference to it in his letters can be noticed as early as 1876.[3]

James's early references to *The Portrait of a Lady* to his family are especially revealing, since they show that from the beginning he felt it would be a major work, a more ambitious novel than any he had yet written. He told his family that, as compared to his previous novels, it would be "as wine unto water"; and thereafter, in the family's letters to him, the projected work is referred to as his "great" novel or as the "wine-and-water novel." James's postponement of the novel appears to have been carefully thought out. He wished to take advantage of his newly won celebrity and the increased demand for his fiction. Between June, 1878, and June, 1880, he produced *Confidence, Hawthorne,* and *Washington Square,* in addition to a group of new stories and a variety of critical articles; and in this way he insured that he would be appearing steadily before the public while he was engaged in writing his longest and most challenging novel.

He began work on *The Portrait of a Lady* in March, 1880, shortly after his arrival in Florence; and when he returned for a stay in London at the beginning of the summer, he had already finished the first installments. In February, 1881, he returned to Italy, and in Venice, in his thirty-eighth year, completed the novel. Twice the length of any of his previous novels, *The Portrait of a Lady* was written very deliberately, each chapter being written twice; and when it was completed in the summer of 1881, its serial publication was already in an advanced stage. *The Portrait of a Lady* was serialized simultaneously in England and America; in England, in *Macmillan's Magazine* (October, 1880–November, 1881), and in America, in the *Atlantic* (November, 1880–December, 1881). From the serialization alone James received $6,000, a considerable sum for the time, with a buying power today of ten times that amount. The novel was published in book form in both England and America in November, 1881, with additional English editions in 1882 and 1883.

Reviews of *The Portrait of a Lady* were generally although not entirely favorable.[4] As James had foreseen, some reviewers objected to the novel's "open" ending, and to its almost purely psychological interest, its relative lack of outward action and incident. Yet a sense that James had produced a work of some remarkable kind can be seen in many of the reviews, both English and American. Despite his reservations, W. C. Brownell called *The Portrait of a Lady* "the most important [novel] Mr. James has thus far written," and "the most eminent example we have had thus far of the realistic art of fiction."[5] John Hay, in the *New York Tribune,* remarked that no "work printed in recent years, on either side of the Atlantic or on either side of the English Channel, surpasses this in seriousness of intention, in easy scope and mastery of material. . . . In every detail of execution this book shows a greater facility, a richer command of resources than any of its predecessors. . . . It is properly to be compared . . . with the greatest and most serious works of the imagination."[6]

The Portrait of a Lady was revised by James on two separate occasions, from the serial to the book version of 1881, and again from the first book version to the final version in the New York Edition (1907–9). The first revision was carefully made but was of a rather marginal nature. Fewer than two hundred passages were retouched, with no single revision exceeding two sentences, and in no case was the novel's theme or structure affected. The later revision, however, contains important changes. Imagery is frequently sharpened, made bolder and more dramatic. Many well-known lines in the novel occurred only in the course of the final revision. In the earlier version, to give only one example, Ralph remarks that "Henrietta, however, is fragrant—Henrietta is decidedly fragrant!"; in revision, more dramatically, the line becomes: "Henrietta, however, does smell of the Future—it almost knocks one down!" (1:131).[7]

Important, too, is the change in the ending. In the late scene between Isabel and Goodwood, in the earlier version, Isabel is assaulted with the sense of being loved: "It wrapped her about; it lifted her off her feet." But the image, in the final version, is elaborated considerably: "She had believed it, but this was different: this was the hot wind of the desert, at the approach of which the others dropped dead, like mere sweet airs of the garden. It wrapped her about; it lifted her off her feet, while the very taste of it, as of something potent, acrid, and strange, forced open her set teeth" (2:434). The imagery of Goodwood's kiss is also altered. The earlier version reads: "His kiss was like a flash of lightning; when it was dark again she was free." But the final version enlarges upon Isabel's sensation in an extended image of "white lightning" and death by drowning: "His kiss was like white lightning, a flash that spread and spread again, and stayed; and it was extraordinarily as if, while she took it, she felt each thing in his hard manhood that had at least pleased her, each aggressive fact of his face, his figure, his presence, justified of its intense identity and made one with this act of possession. So had she heard of those wrecked and under water following a train of images before they sink. But when darkness returned she was free" (2:436). Even the brief, closing conversation between Henrietta and Goodwood is extended to sharpen the point that Henrietta's telling him "just you wait" (2:437) is merely "cheap comfort" rather than grounds for hope. For both style and character shading, the final revision is one of the great successes of the New York Edition, and the text of that edition is the definitive one.

Source and Influence. Anticipations of *The Portrait of a Lady* exist in James's earlier fiction, but the novel was affected, too, by external sources. George Sand's *Indiana* (1832), which James knew well, resembles *The Portrait of a Lady* in some respects, and probably gave two of James's principal characters their names. Isabel, the heroine of *Indiana*, is unhappily married, and in her unhappiness turns at first to the handsome Raymon de Ramière, only to find that he is superficial; by the end she comes to find that the man she loves, after all, is her cousin, Sir Ralph Brown— a shy man, awkward, and introverted, but sincere in his feeling for her. Her protector all along and silent lover, Ralph is united with Isabel at the end in a love based on mutual respect. In *The Portrait of a Lady*, Ralph Touchett and Isabel do not become lovers; but Isabel does make a similarly belated recognition of his worth, and love of a certain kind is claimed.

More striking still are the parallels existing between James's novel and Victor Cherbuliez's *Le Roman d'une Honnête Femme* (1866), or *The Romance of an Honest Woman*. The heroine of the work is named Isabel (she is sometimes called "Isabel the Serious"), and she is evoked in the early section in the imagery of Sleeping Beauty. She lives with her father in a kind of seclusion from the world, and wishes to remain single, preferring her "liberty" to the best of matches. But the Baroness de Ferjeux, described as "worldliness itself," appears rather magically, and proposes an ideal marriage for her, to her nephew, the Marquis de Lestang, a Prince Charming. The marriage arranged, the Baroness exclaims "I trapped the bird." Isabel's marriage to Lestang turns out to be a horror, like Isabel Archer's to Osmond. Like Osmond, too, Lestang lives in a villa on a hilltop with a view below that is "full of enchantment." In time it becomes clear that Isabel's husband has neither love nor respect for her; and Isabel, who above all things prizes her liberty, is condemned to "suffer and be silent" in a house that has a dungeonlike quality. At one point she returns to visit her father, but is too proud to reveal her misery, and actually returns to resume her life with Lestang, to put on the formal appearance of being his happy wife. In its essential character conceptions and its turns of plot, as well as its quality of fairy tale and the chill felt in the entrapment of the freedom-loving "bird," Cherbuliez's once popular but now forgotten novel has very dramatic correspondences with *The Portrait of a Lady*.

Yet more decisive influences still, notably that of Turgenev,[8] are apparent in *The Portrait of a Lady*. In his preface to the novel for the New York Edition, James himself draws attention to Turgenev, reminisces about his meetings with him, recalls his conversation and concern with form in the novel, and remarks that his own conception of *The Portrait of a Lady* began with an image of a character as yet unattached to a particular setting or to other characters, in very much the way that Turgenev began to imagine his tales. The preface, in effect, is an homage to Turgenev, and implies that James felt a particular indebtedness to him in writing *The Portrait of a Lady*.

That indebtedness can be seen in both the texture and form of *The Portrait of a Lady*. The texture, as in Turgenev, is above all delicate, sensitive to the most subtle shadings of tone, of atmosphere, of the poetry of situation. The narrator's voice is understanding, yet implies detachment from the characters involved. Like Turgenev's novels, James's begins with a striking scene in which an "intruder" appears in a particular setting, to create unpredictable complications in the lives of the other characters; and it then sweeps back in time to show the central character in the context of her earlier circumstances. *The Portrait of a Lady* illustrates Turgenev's conception of the "dramatic" novel, which presents its characters through a series of sharply dramatic scenes. Its conclusion has the form of Turgenev's "open" endings, which close with a strong impression that completes the circle of action studied while suggesting that the characters' drama will continue on beyond the ending itself. James's ending, furthermore, is reminiscent specifically of Turgenev's *On the Eve* (1859), which James considered his "greatest triumph." In *On the Eve*, Elena is, as James says, "a girl of will ... calmly ardent and intense,"[9] and the novel becomes a portrait of her, the other characters all serving to set off her character. At the end, she moves away from the orbit of the others to become practically inscrutable in the mystery of her personality, very much as Isabel Archer finally becomes remote and enigmatic in *The Portrait of a Lady*.

James's homage to Turgenev in the preface, however, tends to obscure (perhaps even deliberately conceals) an indebtedness greater even than his, that of George Eliot. In the 1870s, Eliot published two of the greatest novels in English, *Middlemarch* (1873) and *Daniel Deronda* (1876), works James reviewed, and discussed at length in letters to his family and friends; and it was sometime shortly after *Daniel Deronda* was published that James wrote his fragmentary opening for *The Portrait of a Lady*. Isabel Archer, indeed, has the most extraordinary resemblance to both Dorothea Brooke, the heroine of *Middlemarch*, and Gwendolyn Harleth, the heroine of *Daniel Deronda*.[10] Dorothea Brooke has a Puritan strain in her nature that causes her, even if unknowingly, to "seek martyrdom." Her mind is "theoretic"; she is "enamoured of intensity and greatness," and consequently, against the advice of all her friends, she marries an older man whose intellectual accomplishments she has idealized. Her life with the pedantic Mr. Causabon becomes a misery to her, as all of her generous, expansive impulses are constricted within a "chill, colourless, narrowed landscape." Seeking enlargement, she finds a cruel imprisonment in marriage. She suffers in her marriage, unwisely made, in the same way, incurring the same kind of psychological torment, as Isabel Archer.

More remarkable still, however, is Isabel's resemblance to

Gwendolyn Harleth. Like Isabel, Gwendolyn is a young woman with "a certain fierceness of maidenhood" who objects, "with a sort of physical repulsion, to being directly made love to." At the beginning, a "princess in exile," she feels well equipped for the mastery of life, for the management of her own destiny. But she marries unwisely; her husband, Henleigh Grandcourt, has within his nature an egotism Gwendolyn herself possesses, and he reduces her in the course of their marriage to the status of being his creature, a mere reflection of himself. Grandcourt has the same bored lassitude and the ability to inflict intense psychological suffering upon his wife as James's Gilbert Osmond. And as Gwendolyn looks at last to the large-spirited Daniel Deronda for understanding, so Isabel reaches out finally to Ralph Touchett.

Eliot's influence on the character conceptions, and even on the rich, mellow English tone, of *The Portrait of a Lady* is profound. Yet other, significant influences on *The Portrait of a Lady* also exist. Various forms of romance can be noted in it—romantic melodrama and at times even the Gothic mode itself; and the work constantly suggests, in the fall in Italy it depicts, and in its intense encounter between innocence and knowledge, the moral fable dimension of the American prose romance. In *The Portrait of a Lady* realism and romance engage each other as in a debate between opposing allegiances, an allegiance to experience in all of its concreteness and finitude, and an allegiance to the intensities and recognitions that belong to pure inner being.

The Use of Fairy Tale

The Portrait of a Lady shows James in the fullness of his powers. The sheer beauty, grace, and assurance of the writing, almost startling in the opening description of Gardencourt, and sustained for five-hundred pages, reveal James at a new level of achievement as a prose stylist; and the richness of his character portraits and intensity of his engagement with his subject are of a kind that belong to history-making novels. *The Portrait of a Lady* is history-making literally. The opening account of Gardencourt, in which a densely solid actuality has begun to dissolve into psychological atmosphere, shows literary impressionism at a high stage of development.[11] And Isabel's chapter-length meditative vigil, projected in a long, dramatic interior monologue, lays the foundations of the stream-of-consciousness novel of Joyce, Dorothy Richardson, and Virginia Woolf.

In one of its dimensions, *The Portrait of a Lady* is James's as yet most elaborately conceived fairy tale. His use of fairy tale was evident in *Watch and Ward, Roderick Hudson, The American,* and *The Europeans*; but in *The Portrait of a Lady* it is wedded to his conception of the American girl, who becomes a figure of size to sustain a fairy tale of size. The appearance of her aunt Touchett before Isabel at the Albany house is a fairy-tale visitation, a more wondrous materialization than that of Felix Young before Gertrude Wentworth. Like Gertrude, Isabel has been poring over a book, in this case in a secluded room called the "office," where her inner or romantic life is lived. Previously a "princess" in the small room of a provincial house, she now becomes a princess in the great world, as Lydia Touchett transports her to a splendid country house in England.

Upon her arrival, Gardencourt seems to her, as she says, like something out of a novel; Lockleigh, the neighboring estate of Lord Warburton, is like "a castle in a legend" (1:108). With an effect that is larger than life, the eligible young lord of Lockleigh proposes to her on their third meeting, and more wondrously still, she refuses him. Her aunt takes her to live with her in a habitation becoming a princess—a palace in Florence. Before long she comes into a marvelous bequest, enabling her to meet the requirements of her imagination. In Florence, however, the princess meets Gilbert Osmond, "a demoralized prince in exile" (1:352) and, most unwisely, she marries him. Soon her "open" world is confined within his "closed" one in their life in a Roman palazzo, having the cold, cruel associations of a dungeon. Several men attempt to rescue her, including the persistent Goodwood, described in the imagery of a modern knight, whose eyes seem "to shine through the vizard of a helmet" (1:218). But at the end no one at all can save the princess—except herself.

Development Through Patterns of Imagery

The emotive range of the novel is enlarged by fairy tale, but it is deepened also by James's persistent use of symbolic forms and of figurative language. Houses, for example, are used in a way that incorporates them into the novel's symbolic action. Isabel's house in Albany is not merely a frame, like the Wentworth house in *The Europeans* that connotes a cultural idea, but is deeply part of her psychology. Gardencourt, as the different parts of the name imply, embraces a range of alternative values—both nature and civilization, innocence and knowledge, freedom and responsibility. The whole question of choice and perspective is implied. Osmond's villa set on a hilltop expresses him, his aloofness from the rest of mankind; it expresses him even in details, in its deceptive, masklike facade, its windows that "defy the world to look in" (1:326). The Palazzo Roccanera, "in the very heart of Rome (2:100), is the outward form of the blighting of aspiration belonging to the human past that Isabel experiences inwardly. In the Palazzo Roccanera, Isabel even thinks of Osmond's mind in the imagery of a house: "She had lived with it, she had lived *in* it almost—it appeared to have become her habitation. . . . It was the house of darkness, the house of dumbness, the house of suffocation" (2:194, 196).

James had used image patterns to reinforce his theme in such earlier novels as *Roderick Hudson*, but in *The Portrait of a Lady* he carries the use of imagery a step further by making it constantly reflect on Isabel's consciousness. In an early image that later expands, Isabel's inner life is compared to a garden. "She was always planning out her development," James writes, "desiring her perfection, observing her progress. Her nature had, in her conceit, a certain gardenlike quality, a suggestion of perfume and murmuring boughs, of shady bowers and lengthening vistas, which made her feel that introspection was, after all, an exercise in the open air, and that a visit to the recesses of one's spirit was harmless when one returned from it with a lapful of roses. But she was often reminded that there were other gardens in the world than those of her remarkable soul, and that there were moreover a great many places which were not gardens at all—only dusky pestiferous tracts, planted thick with ugliness and misery" (1:72). This imagery hints at illusion, in the impression it gives that Isabel's assumptions, while very noble, have as yet been untested, that her familiarity with the world has been limited. Her idealizing habit is often expressed in other garden images. When, early in the work, she thinks of Osmond, she pictures him with his little daughter in "a formal Italian garden" (1:400). The terrace of Osmond's villa is a "narrow garden" (1:326) that looks down upon a valley landscape having a high aesthetic finish, a landscape with a "gardenlike culture and nobleness of outline" (1:380). Isabel weds herself to this view of nature and civilization triumphantly reconciled when she marries Osmond.

Garden imagery is elaborated to become the novel's dominant metaphor. Contemplating her suave friend, Isabel wanders, "as by the wrong side of a private garden, round the enclosed talents, accomplishments, aptitudes of Madame Merle" (1:270). When Lord Warburton proposes, his words are uttered with a candor "that was like the fragrance straight in her face ... of she knew not what strange gardens" (1:152). As Isabel stands by an open window in a room of the Palazzo Crescentini, during a reverie in which the recent events leading up to her decision to marry Osmond pass in review, the "bright air of the garden" below fills the room with "warmth and perfume" (2:31). Shortly afterwards, she enters the garden itself, captured in the imagery of Eden as it is pictured in Milton's *Paradise Lost*, and here Ralph speaks of the sorrow he feels to see that she has "fallen." In the marriage she enters into, Isabel finds her spirit annexed by Osmond's own, mean one. "Her mind," James remarks, "was to be his—attached to his own like a small garden-plot to a deer-park" (2:200). It is by the garden bench on the grounds of the Touchett house that

Warburton proposes, that Goodwood importunes, that Goodwood, in kissing Isabel in the climactic scene, triggers psychological terror in the garden of her mind.

Having focal importance, too, is the imagery of art objects, which contributes to the delineation of character. Visiting the picture gallery at Gardencourt for the first time, Isabel sees the paintings on its walls as "vague squares of rich colour" (1:161); but near the end, visiting it again, she lingers before a Bonington, and the distinctness of her sense of it measures the growth that has occurred in her since her first appearance at Gardencourt. At various times, furthermore, characters are likened to art objects. Osmond's beard has been "cut in the manner of the portraits of the sixteenth century" (1:328), and his fastidious appearance suggests "that he was a gentleman who studied style" (1:328). He is described as a "fine, gold coin," an "elegant complicated medal struck off for a special occasion" (1:328). Ned Rosier imagines Pansy as a Dresden-china shepherdess, and as "an Infanta of Velasquez" (2:108). Ralph thinks of Isabel's "passionate force" at play as being "finer than the finest work of art—than a Greek bas-relief, than a great Titian, than a Gothic cathedral" (1:86). Osmond regards her as a work of art, too, but only after her vital spirit has been subdued and rendered inert under his supervision and placed in his collection. Her imagination of a keen purity is a prized item, and Osmond thinks of it as a silver plate: "he could tap her imagination with his knuckle and make it ring" (2:79). But what is notable in this image is that Isabel as a silver plate has a purely passive function, to "ring" under the pressure of Osmond's knuckle.

Almost all of the characters, at one time or another, are given some kind of definition through a comparison of them to art objects. Even a shabby Florentine footboy might have "been 'put in' by the brush of a Longhi or a Goya" (1:387). Madame Merle, with her hair styled somehow "classically," is compared to a statue of Juno or Niobe; and Mrs. Touchett has the dry, definite face of a relief figure "in a fresco of Ghirlandaio's" (1:372). In certain cases a character is revealed by an art object, or given a fused identity with it. As Osmond reproduces in watercolor from a plate the likeness of a Roman coin, one has the sense that he has been shown nakedly, as if his soul itself were a coin, and as if multiple planes of refraction existed between him and anything real. Madame Merle, most of all, is like some consummately fashioned work of art; but in a late scene her imperfection is implied by a delicate coffee cup on a mantle shelf, a choice object that is seemingly perfect yet betrays the existence of a crack. As Madame Merle holds the cup in her hand distractedly, she wails: "Have I been so vile all for nothing?" (2:338); and at this moment the flawed cup becomes the symbol of her nature and moral failure.

Ultimately, the pervasive art object imagery raises questions of values. Both Ralph and Osmond are connoisseurs, but their attitudes toward art, and by extension toward life, are significantly different. Unlike Ralph, Osmond cannot smile at himself. His self-importance tolerates no levity, and he permits no personal freedom in those close to him, who become mere satellites of his egotism. He makes art superior to life, as Ralph does not. Ralph wishes to set Isabel "free," as Osmond wishes to deny her even the smallest remnant of her individuality. At one point Osmond remarks to Isabel: "Don't you remember my telling you that one ought to make one's life a work of art? ... it was exactly what you seemed to me to be trying to do with your own" (2:15). But in attempting to make life a work of art, Isabel is guilty of the kind of thinking seen in Osmond, who regards art as something that exists apart from life and is superior to it.

But, in fact, a large number of image patterns affect the work and guide its theme. The imagery of eyes is particularly prominent. Goodwood has "clear-burning eyes" containing a spirit that is "like some tireless watcher at a window" (1:162); and Lord Warburton's eyes are "charged with the light of a passion that had sifted itself clear of the baser parts of emotion—the heat, the violence, the unreason—and that burned as steadily as a lamp in a windless place" (1:148). In perhaps the most spectacular image, added in revision, the Misses Molyneux, the sisters of Lord Warburton, have "eyes like the balanced basins, the circles of 'ornamental water,' set in parterres, among the geraniums" (1:104). In the "grey depths" of their eyes, Isabel sees the reflection of everything she has rejected in rejecting Lord Warburton—the calm, unagitated, traditional nature of English life. Henrietta Stackpole's eyes are like large polished buttons that, in the remarkable directness and fixity of their gaze, make Ralph feel vaguely dishonored or violated. Henrietta, particularly, calls attention to the idea of seeing that is limited to surfaces—of seeing without understanding. Her journalistic observations of Europe for the *New York Interviewer* are made wholly from without, with all that cannot be grasped quickly, the less penetrable human dimension, left out. She is guilty of the kind of perception of which Ralph accuses Isabel—of seeing without feeling.

Many other image patterns, notably of water, birds, flight, and wings, are pronounced in the work. Water would suggest life and experience, as it clearly does when Ralph wishes to tie Isabel round his neck "as a life-preserver" (1:11); but sometimes it is associated with hazard or even death, as when Henrietta fears that Isabel is drifting "right out to sea" (1:170). At other times (James's allusions to *The Tempest* are relevant in this respect), water is associated with rebirth and redemption. Both Daniel Touchett and Ralph die during rain storms, and there is some suggestion, in Ralph's death particularly, of redemptive possibilities for Isabel. Isabel's aspiration is frequently figured in the imagery of birds and flight. James calls her a "winged spirit" (2:160), and Ralph tells her: "spread your wings; rise above the ground" (1:319). During her first stay in Rome, Isabel's imagination soars from the Roman past to her own future "in a single flight and now hovered in slow circles over the nearer and richer field" (1:415).

But with this flight imagery, one notices image patterns of keys (Isabel even has a sister named Mrs. Keyes), of locks and bolts, often used with an implication that would discourage flight or make it impossible. When Osmond declares his love, Isabel seems to hear "the slipping of a fine bolt—backward-forward, she couldn't have said which" (2:18). The hazard of entrapment is also figured in the imagery of steel traps and cages. When Lord Warburton proposes, Isabel moves back from the opportunity offered "even as some wild, caught creature in a vast cage" (1:153). The caging of the beautiful striver is enacted through a vast play of dramatic imagery that, far more than in any of James's previous novels, takes the reader into the consciousness of the central character, and through Isabel's highly focused consciousness James's "interior" novel really comes into being.

Reservations About Characterization

Yet although constantly concerned with Isabel's consciousness, the novel does not take place wholly within it. *The Ambassadors*, written two decades later, is narrated consistently from Lambert Strether's point of view, and is a history of his consciousness; but in *The Portrait of a Lady*, two entire chapters take place outside the limits of what Isabel can know, and James himself sometimes intrudes to remark on her illusions. She is, however, always central to the work, the other characters grouping about her. One of the characters, Caspar Goodwood, exists only in his relation to her; and seems, indeed, like a specter in her mind made manifest. He is not delineated socially to any extent, has a fitful existence in his sudden appearances, and none at all when he departs. The Countess Gemini is more fully portrayed than Goodwood, but she suffers somewhat from having a rather rigidly assigned role to play, that of being Osmond's contrasting sibling, as Mrs. Penniman is Dr. Sloper's. Osmond and the countess have a partly American parentage (their mother having confronted the beauty of Europe with a tremulous idealism), but their upbringing has been European; they suggest a corrupt mingling of the new world and the old, an American idealistic impulse gone wrong. In both, in their contrasting ways, one notices a failed sense of proportion. As Osmond has a morbidly exaggerated sense of privacy and exclusiveness, the countess has no sense of privacy at all. Her extramarital affairs are public knowledge, and she is delighted by the idea of Henrietta's publishing her confidences in her newspaper, insisting even that she mention that her husband, the count, cannot read, and asking her to be sure to give their names. Within her limits, the Countess Gemini is an engaging character, belonging to a type of eccentric matron James does to perfection. Her revelation to Isabel of Pansy's illegitimate birth provides a "big" scene, but she seems to exist almost entirely for the sake of making this disclosure.

If one were to look for any weakness in characterization in a work in which character portraiture is a particular strength, one might notice the effect on characterization of James's handling of sexuality. Osmond is a great study in perversity, and one of the great characters in James's fiction, but an oddity clings to him. Like Dr. Sloper, he is enclosed totally within himself, a being of such chilled reactions to life that it is difficult to imagine his sexual partnership with Isabel, or their having produced a child. Aloof from others, as well as from the grossly physical, Osmond seems never to have been capable of falling in love or having an "affair," although an important earlier one with Madame Merle is claimed. Grandcourt, in *Daniel Deronda*, resembles Osmond in many respects, but he is more fully accounted for in his perversity. He has the emotional coldness and sharp cruelty of a smugly aristocratic English breeding, and in addition the sadistic nature of his sexuality is quite apparent. Osmond, on the other hand, seems to exist without a sexual nature, being sheer, perverse intelligence.

An element of ambiguity can also be noticed in Ralph Touchett. As a consumptive he is "honorably" disqualified from an active life; yet his illness also suggests an inability to function sexually. In a number of passages, he is shown with his hands in his pockets, an almost characteristic gesture with him that was also the gesture of Robert Acton, indicating his paralysis through sexual fear. Furthermore, Ralph's incapacity is accompanied by interests that are deeply aesthetic, and that make him reminiscent of a line of earlier artist figures thinly disguised, like Ford and Mason. His conception as a bona fide consumptive on the one hand, and as an artist surrogate (or even as a version of James himself) on the other, creates a blurred sense of him.

Ralph's death at Gardencourt is especially perplexing, for in this passage the reader is asked to share James's sense that Ralph's

avoidance of physical intimacy represents a form of love far
nobler than sexual love could be. "And remember this," he tells
Isabel as he dies, "that if you've been hated, you've also been
loved." To this, in revision, James adds: " 'Ah, but Isabel—*adored*!'
he just audibly and lingeringly breathed" (2:417). His fineness is not lost on Isabel, who cries: "Oh my brother!" In order
to achieve intensity, James resorts to melodramatic conventions, the
deathbed scene of the stage in which the character who is dying
is ennobled and fully valued by others at last. The scene is not
crudely melodramatic, but its sources in melodrama do raise a
doubt in the reader's mind about Ralph. Is he really all that James
would have him seem? Or does his finer love than a physical one
contain a rationalization of his inability to enter into sexual experience? D. H. Lawrence would have had some interesting words
for Ralph's aesthetic "love in the head," and the reader, generally,
shies away from the valuation of Ralph that is urged.

The Portrait of Isabel

The Portrait of a Lady is, nevertheless, a work of remarkable
power and subtlety, a novel in which the most concentrated focus
upon Isabel yet admits of elaborate complexity. Complexity is
announced at the opening with Mrs. Touchett's cryptic telegram,
notifying Mr. Touchett and Ralph of her arrival with a niece. The
wording of the telegram has a scrambled effect, making its meaning unclear. The last words, "quite independent," are particularly
confusing, since they admit of many interpretations; it is not clear
who is independent, or in what sense the term is used. The implication is given that absolute terms or ideas become meaningful only
in relation to referents, which place limits on their meaning or
define them. Isabel is very fond of her freedom, her independence,
but these absolutes must be defined concretely by experience—by
the relationships into which she is put, and the choices she is
compelled to make. On her first appearance, she declares the importance to her of her liberty; and shortly afterwards, she announces that it is "not absolutely necessary to suffer; we were not

made for that" (1:65). But her assumptions have yet to be tested.

Isabel is measured, among others, by her aunt Touchett, since she, too, is very independent, so fond of her freedom that, although remaining Daniel Touchett's wife in name, she is almost wholly detached from him. She has few commitments of any kind; her traveling from place to place, settling for a time here and for a time there, suggests a life lived without fixed commitments. Her material means enable her to follow her whims, but such freedom leads her finally into meaningless idiosyncrasy. When she first appears at the Albany house she announces: "I haven't a delusion!" (1:32); but it is her misfortune that she hasn't. She makes on her first appearance a large worldly presence, but as the novel progresses she actually seems to shrink, to be revealed as an obstinately narrow old woman who is peripheral to everything. "Isabel came at last," James remarks, "to have a kind of undemonstrable pity for her; there seemed something so dreary in the condition of a person whose nature had, as it were, so little surface—offered so limited a face to the accretions of human contact. Nothing tender, nothing sympathetic, had ever a chance to fasten upon it— no wind-sown blossom, no familiar softening moss. Her offered, her passive extent, in other words, was about that of a knife-edge" (1:317). As Ralph lies dying, Mrs. Touchett tells Isabel "It has not been a successful life" (2:405); she is speaking of her son in this passage, but her words apply more justly to herself. Lacking any enrichment of consciousness, even the suffering that might have come from a great mistake, she is like certain of James's later characters who are defeated more terribly than anyone in their failure to have been touched by life, to have shared in "the common doom," to have lived. Isabel sees her at the end as "an old woman without memories. Her little sharp face looked tragical!" (2:407).

Mrs. Touchett's independence leads, in a sense, to the loss of her life; and the question is raised if Isabel's insistence upon her independence will not lead to the loss of hers. Isabel even wonders at one point, with a twinge of fear, if her insistence on her freedom may not lead to some desert place of pride and isolation. Certainly she is vulnerable, since pride and isolation are part of her character. Moreover, Osmond very strikingly represents pride and isolation, even pride *in* isolation, and in him one has a morbid reflection of Isabel. Her motives in marrying him have much to do with her pride in her separateness from others. Her travels in the Middle East are a kind of triumphal, processional conquest of time and human experience through a superior spectatorship. On her return, she chooses to marry Osmond, a choice in which there is to be no relinquishment of her pride in her detachment. She reflects that Osmond "was like a sceptical voyager strolling on the beach while he waited for the tide, looking seaward yet not putting to sea. It was in all this she found her occasion. She would launch his boat for him; she would be his providence; it would be a good thing to love him" (2:192). To stand apart, playing the role of providence with another's life, is the apotheosis of Isabel's pride.

In her attitude of detachment, Isabel is measured by a number of other characters, including Henrietta Stackpole, whose role as a newspaper correspondent abroad makes her preeminently an observer-spectator. Moreover, her comic name, Stackpole, suggests a jerrybuilt or awkwardly improvised altitude, and it is from a height that she looks upon the various social arrangements from which she herself stands apart. Different as they are, Isabel and Henrietta have many traits in common, and their careers run parallel through much of the work. Isabel is fiercely virginal, refusing offers of matrimony, and Henrietta is a spinster. Both are questors who wish to see "for themselves" and to know everything; and they are ardent. Isabel is courageous, and admires the courage of Henrietta: "She was brave: she went into cages, she flourished lashes" (1:127). Both are highly "theoretical"; it is by her jingoist notions that Henrietta gauges Europe, criticizing its manners and customs for failing to meet an American standard. She already has a conception of Ralph as a decadent expatriate before she even comes to know him. Both Isabel and Henrietta have restless, agitated consciences that will not permit them an easy acceptance of life. Isabel rejects Lord Warburton because his profoundly settled place in English life would smother her, and Henrietta travels restlessly, with notebook in hand. Isabel is pursued by several men, Henrietta is courted by Mr. Bantling.

Later in the work, however, their careers diverge. A constant critic of Ralph, Henrietta comes finally to appreciate him, to realize that her theories about him have been superficial; their mellowing relationship is one of the fine things in the novel. More than that, the barriers between Henrietta and British life begin to come down, and Henrietta actually engages herself to marry the English Mr. Bantling. Richard Poirier has described Henrietta as a character who is "fixed" rather than "free" to develop; but such a typing of her hardly seems justified. Limited she obviously is, but she is not wholly a comic figure. She makes some of the most pertinent comments about Isabel in the novel, and in its later part she grows in understanding. Her engagement to Bantling, after an acquaintance with him of five years, represents a choice in marriage as successful as Isabel's has been disastrous. The ardent chauvinist even comes, for the first time, to qualify her patriotism by acknowledging that American preoccupation with "brain-power" may be exaggerated, a recognition that indicates James's blessing on her as a character who has achieved larger awareness. In her accommodation with the institutional life of England, Henrietta will not cease to be herself, but she will relinquish some of the absolutism that has been part of her former separateness from others.

Isabel's reaction to Henrietta's engagement is quite revealing. "Henrietta, after all," Isabel reflects, "had confessed herself human and feminine, Henrietta whom she had hitherto regarded as a light keen flame, a disembodied voice. It was a disappointment to find she had personal susceptibilities, that she was subject to common passions, and that her intimacy with Mr. Bantling had not been completely original. There was a want of originality in her marrying him—there was even a kind of stupidity, and for a moment, to Isabel's sense, the dreariness of the world took on a deeper tinge" (2:400). Isabel has admired Henrietta for being a "disembodied voice," a flame, rather than for being of human substance; and she protests against Henrietta's admission to susceptibilities that are *personal*, that do not support a relation to life that is, in her perfectly chosen Emersonian word, "original."

It is against the background of Emerson and the New England Transcendentalists that Isabel's ideals and striving have been sketched. It is significant that when she is depicted early in the Albany house, she is shown as a solitary, engaged in reading a history of German idealist philosophy (described as a "sandy plain" or desert)—the source of Transcendentalism. She is already identified with an attitude that is abstract, idealized, remote—the qualities of temperament, as recorded in various essays, that James ascribed to Emerson. Isabel has an Emersonian self-culture, a radical innocence that rejects suffering and endorses self-trust. James describes her attitudes with unmistakable echoes of Emerson: "She had a theory that . . . one should be of the best, should be conscious of a fine organisation . . . should move in a realm of light, of inspiration gracefully chronic. . . . She had a fixed determination to regard the world as a place of brightness, of free expansion, or irresistible action" (1:68). Even her motives in rejecting Lord Warburton are expressed in an Emersonian idiom: "He appeared to demand of her something that no one else, as it were, had presumed to do. What she felt was that a territorial, a political, a social magnate had conceived the design of drawing her into the system in which he rather invidiously lived and moved. A certain instinct, not imperious, but persuasive, told her to resist—murmured to her that virtually she had a system and an orbit of her own" (1:144). In "The American Scholar," Emerson uses an almost identical vocabulary, declaring that it would be better never to see a book "than to be warped by its attraction clean out of my own orbit, and made a satellite instead of a system."

Exposed to actual experience, Isabel's assumptions and judgments often prove faulty; objective reality is somewhat unreal to her. The person she had admired most, even idolized, is her father, a man with a "large way" of looking at life. Yet he has, in fact, provided her with an erratic education, one that some found no education at all; gambled so freely and mismanaged his affairs so badly that

she is left with an inheritance far smaller than she might have
expected. Isabel believes that he had kept "the unpleasant" away
from her, but it was present whether or not she had been able to
see it. Isabel's relatively weak sense of concrete reality is brought
out in a conversation with Madame Merle. Madame Merle insists
that the individual is defined by the envelope of circumstances in
which he exists. The house in which one lives, the garments one
wears, the books one reads are all expressive. Isabel protests that
nothing expresses her except "her self," which cannot be defined
by "things." The exchange reveals them both. Madame Merle's
tragedy is in living only for "things," in having no inner self, no
life apart from the worldly role she adopts and the use she is
able to make of "things" and people. Isabel, on the other hand, is
tragically shortsighted in being unable to recognize that "things"
are indeed real and impose limits on the self. It is partly in her
belief that the money she inherits is a superfluity and not part of
her essential self that she marries the fortune-hunting Osmond.

Isabel's inner self, upon which she places royal value, is, furthermore, not all that it seems. It is not merely a place of light, but
of light and darkness both, as she is vaguely aware when she compares herself with the Misses Molyneux and wonders for a moment if there is perhaps not something morbid in her own nature.
Her curiously dual nature is implied by the "double house" in Albany, where she is found in the early part of the work. As a child,
Isabel thinks of the house, which has two entrances, one of them
locked and unused, as "romantic," since it is full of undefined
presences from the past. Her favorite area of the house is an
unused room beyond the library called "the office," a place with
the musty smell of discarded furniture—"victims," as she likes to
imagine them, of injustice. It is a place of "mysterious melancholy,"
reached properly from the bolted and "condemned" door that had
once opened onto the street. James remarks that Isabel had never
opened the bolted door, had never assured herself that the "vulgar
street" lay beyond: "She had no wish to look out, for this would
have interfered with her theory that there was a strange, unseen

place on the other side—a place which became to the child's imagination, according to its different moods, a region of delight or of terror" (1:30).

As the most unfrequented quarter of the house, and the most remote from active life, the room suggests the inner recesses of young Isabel's soul. It is a place of imagination having, like its discarded furniture, a melancholy cast. In one of its connotations the word "office" indicates a world of the spirit, since in an ecclesiastical sense an "office" is a prayer, or form of communion or worship, as in the "Office of the Dead"; and the world with which Isabel frequently communes is more recognizably that of the dead than of the living. When Mrs. Touchett comes upon her in this room, Isabel explains: "I like places in which things have happened— even if they're sad things. A great many people have died here; the place has been full of life"; and Mrs. Touchett replies astutely: "Is that what you call being full of life?" (1:35).

Isabel has within her nature a strange ambivalence; she declares her belief in brightness and free expansion, yet withdraws to dark corners and engages in melancholy introspection. In the Albany house, young Isabel hears from the open windows of the Dutch House school across the street "the hum of childish voices repeating the multiplication table—an incident in which the elation of liberty and the pain of exclusion were indistinguishably mingled" (1:29). That they are indistinguishable implies that she cannot tell one from the other. Later in her life, when she must make choices, she cannot distinguish elation from pain. The anguished experience of Goodwood's kiss sends her rushing back to Osmond, to find a new elation in suffering.

The Question of the Ending

No feature of *The Portrait of a Lady* has been debated more frequently than its ending. One group of James's critics, including Richard Chase and Richard Poirier, regard Isabel's return to Osmond as an act of folly that brings her at last to the point of tragedy. Yet other critics, including Lyall Powers, reject this interpretation of a tragic Isabel, and see her return to Osmond as an act of "responsibility" and "wisdom." Powers, in particular, regards *The Portrait of a Lady* as the story of a fall and redemption. Isabel is right, he thinks, to reject Goodwood at the end, since he tempts her with a spurious "freedom," a form of escapism. She returns to Rome to accept responsibility for another life, Pansy's, and in doing so is reborn in a selfless love shown to her by Ralph, whose generous vision of love is evoked as Christ-like. Neither of these readings is perhaps entirely satisfactory, but the Powers interpretation of a return to salvation,[12] which has gained currency and been restated in many recent essays, is particularly vulnerable. It is an interpretation that a close reading of the novel will not support.

To assume, as Powers rather casually does, that Isabel at the end has now understood the errors she has made in the past and become "wise" is to assume a great deal. An early passage reveals her. When Henrietta asks Isabel if she knows where she is drifting, she exclaims: "No, I haven't the least idea, and I find it very pleasant not to know. A swift carriage, of a dark night, rattling with four horses over roads that one can't see—that's my idea of happiness" (1:235). Her words echo the closing lines of Goethe's autobiography, *Dichtung und Wahrheit*, in which he sees himself at the reins of "a light car of destiny," hurtling along uncertain roads, unaware of his destination or even of whence he came. The image dramatizes Goethe's sense of the will toward self-perfection as an urgent and powerful force of nature, a force superior to reason. This Goethean sense of heroic self-perfection is also in Isabel, and it is felt in her still at the end. She returns to England demoralized by her marriage to Osmond, and her spirits droop as she thinks of Henrietta's having, in her mind, "given up" her independence. She passes through the painful experience of Ralph's dying in her arms, and is then confronted by Goodwood, whose kiss seems to her, in her nightmarelike experience of it, as a final attempt to force her to surrender her sense of self. It is shortly after this incident that the protest that has been gathering in her finds expression, that she is galvanized into action, that she turns again to Italy with renewed strength and determination to reinstate her self-conception. She returns to Osmond to become Pansy's protectress, to feel once more the force of her individuality, even if in martyrdom. She returns not in a Christian conversion to selflessness, one would submit, but in a renewal of heroic striving.

The final scene with Goodwood can be interpreted in various ways; his urging Isabel to leave Osmond need not be seen as an attempt to lure her from responsibility by a form of escapism. It is true that he tells her "We can do absolutely as we please.... The world's all before us" (2:435), and that the limitless freedom of which he speaks is not literally possible. But their future would still be open, even if not absolutely. Moreover, the lines echo those in *Paradise Lost* when Adam and Eve must leave Eden to enter the imperfect world. Isabel would, in effect, be leaving the Eden of her abstract relation to life to take her place in the common condition of mankind. Even the imagery of Isabel's nightmare when Goodwood kisses her can be seen as an indication of her horror at having to confront experience on a real rather than theoretical basis. If the water in which she feels herself drowning suggests life, and the blinding illumination of the "white lightning" reality, then Isabel's recoil and subsequent return to Osmond would imply an escape from reality. What is perhaps more significant than whether or not she should reject Goodwood (who is not entirely attractive) is the implication that she has never before had to confront him as being *real* rather than an emanation of her remarkable soul.

Powers's interpretation of the ending is weak, finally, in its contention that Isabel becomes "responsible" in returning to stand beside Pansy. It seems hardly to have occurred to Powers that in returning to aid and protect Pansy, Isabel is adopting a highly abstract role. In this return, she is still enacting the part of Diana, who was not only the goddess of chastity and the hunt, but also protectress of the young. It is in a world, above all, of elevated abstraction that Isabel will live in shielding Pansy from life, just as, ironically, Osmond removes her from the sphere of life by placing her in a convent, and making her a reflection of himself.

Pansy is herself a kind of abstraction—a little angel of heaven, as she is called. A "daddy's girl" if there ever was one, sheltered and kept spotless, she seems at the age of twenty like a small girl. Her romance with Ned Rosier has about it so little of the physical that it has a disembodied quality. With his rosy cheeks, daintiness, and bibelots, Rosier is hardly grossly physical; he has not even the grossness of a sex drive. Together Pansy and Rosier make a "pretty" picture of innocent child-adults, and for them, in defense of such purity and preserved innocence, Isabel is prepared to lay down her life. What is striking is that what Isabel sees in Pansy is herself— she, who had been another "daddy's girl," kept apart from life by her father in a world of her romantic imaginings and her "theories," which even at the end she refuses to relinquish.

But to say that she is an illusionist is not to say that she is a figure like Emma Bovary, an empty being of sordid illusion. The ardor of Isabel's innocence and striving give her a stature that other characters in the novel (such as her sisters) do not have at all, and it is clear that James feels for her more deeply than for any of his characters of the earlier novels. There is, furthermore, an implication that although Isabel's return to Osmond brings her to the point of tragedy, hope may yet exist for her. She is still young when the novel ends, and one part of her experience has yet to be gauged. *The Portrait of a Lady* is not, in any strict sense, a "religious" novel. When Ralph is dying he tells Isabel that life is better than death, for in life there is love, while in death there is none. These words, which are James's as much as Ralph's, do not imply a belief in a Christian afterlife, an eternal salvation in God's love. Yet James invokes something like religious emotion, or a religious sense of life, at certain points in the work, and particularly in Ralph's death and legacy to Isabel. Ralph *does* have Christ-like connotations in his dying on the third day of his suffering, with the words "Keep me in your heart" (2:413) on his lips; and the sacramental aspect of his death is meant to suggest that for the heroine, although erring in pride and self-centeredness, there is yet hope of redemption through the power of loving.

Isabel's "garden" implies a remote, inviolable innocence and separateness from others; but the flower imagery associated with Ralph has an entirely different connotation. "His serenity," James writes, "was but the array of wild flowers niched in his ruin" (1:54). These wild flowers have grown out of deprivation, loss, and suffering—a self-forgetful, reverent love for the being of others. When Isabel rushes back to Osmond, she is still gripped by the absolutist ideals that she would impose on life, and it is not yet certain that Ralph's "wild flowers," his legacy to her, will take root in her life. But they *may*. A long life yet lies ahead of her, and it is certain to be one in which there will be suffering. The love she comes to feel for Ralph at the end of the novel is deeply *personal*, is intimate rather than heroic; and it may lead to a deepened humanity in her. Ralph, certainly, will dwell in her thoughts. At the end, the perspective shifts from Isabel as Ralph's "life-preserver," to Ralph as Isabel's.

An important word in *The Portrait of a Lady* is "patience." While Isabel sits in the "office" of the Albany house, a "crude, cold rain" falls outside, and the spring season, the spring renewal, seems to her "a cynical, insincere appeal—to patience" (1:31). The word recurs and is, in fact, the final one of the novel, as Henrietta tells Goodwood to wait, "as if she had given him now the key to patience" (2:438). Daniel Touchett's patience has been rewarded when the novel opens. He had originally bought Gardencourt, grumbling at "its ugliness, its antiquity, its incommodity" (1:3), but at the end of twenty years has developed a fine aesthetic appreciation of it—a perspective achieved only after much time. Isabel's ardent conscience, a conscience that cannot rest, interferes with an attainment of patience; and the question that is raised and left dangling at the end is whether she can yet find this patience that is to be crucial to her life.

Like the word "patience," the word "key" is used frequently, and is highly relevant. When Isabel learns that Henrietta will settle in England, she remarks: "You will at last ... see something of the inner life"; and Henrietta replies: "That's the key to the mystery, I believe" (2:400). The key to the mystery of *The Portrait of a Lady* is the inner life, the receptive spirit, in which ego has been subdued, that brings the imagination of loving—as James calls it in the novel and in its preface—into being. Whether Isabel will attain to this disinterested imagination of loving is left unresolved. To repeat, there is no return to salvation; there are only "terms" provided for the reader, and a dramatic crisis created. In this boldest of James's endings, the reader is forced to put himself in Isabel's place, to see beyond what is strictly known, to take part in a drama that is critical to Isabel's life and is, indeed, inward.

Chapter Eight

The Bostonians :
James Among the Reformers

Background

Genesis and Text. In October, 1881, with *The Portrait of a Lady* completed, James crossed the Atlantic to visit his family, whom he had not seen in five years, and after spending the autumn with them he then visited in New York City, Philadelphia, and Washington, D.C.[1] In Washington, however, in January, 1882, and while staying with the Henry Adamses, he received word suddenly of his mother's death. After her funeral, James remained in Boston for nearly five months, returning to London only in May, 1882, on his father's urging that he resume his usual life. Yet hardly six months later he was notified that his father was dying, and he returned once again to America, arriving only just after his father's death. Partly because the elder James named him executor of his estate, James stayed on in Boston for nearly nine months, after which, in August, 1883, he returned to live permanently in England. The years between 1881 and 1883 were lived by James in the shadow of death in the family; and it was a time for him, generally, of fatigue and demoralization. His attitude toward America during this time, as recorded in his journal, makes him seem like a stranger in his own homeland. Boston, he wrote, meant nothing to him; he did not even dislike it. The whole experience of his return to death seemed like a dream—"like a very painful dream."[2]

It was during this time that James formed his conception of *The Bostonians*; its plot outline, entered into his notebooks in April, 1883, was written while he was living on Beacon Hill, and is a transcription of the outline he sent at that time to R. W. Gilder, editor of the *Century Magazine*, with a proposal for its serialization. Arrangements were not worked out with Gilder, however, until over a year later. James began the actual composition of the novel in London in August, 1884, and in October of that year submitted the first installment to the magazine, which began serialization of it in its February, 1885, issue. The first installment, as it happened, appeared in the same issue with other major works of American realism—with the fourth installment of Howells's *The Rise of Silas Lapham*, and the "Royalty on the Mississippi" chapter of Twain's *Adventures of Huckleberry Finn*. *The Bostonians* appeared on a monthly basis in the magazine from February, 1885, to February, 1886, and early in 1886 it was published in book form in both America and England.

Unfortunately, the publication of *The Bostonians* proved a serious setback in James's career. The book sold very poorly; in addition, James's American publisher, James R. Osgood, from whom he was to have received a fee of $4,000 for serial rights, went bankrupt. Macmillan, his English publisher, brought out the book in America, in place of Osgood & Co., but in the complicated transaction James lost the income he had expected from the novel's serialization. *The Bostonians*, furthermore, met with a hostile reception by American reviewers; of all the reviews, not one was favorable.[3] Rather than being shocked by James's irreverent treatment of Boston, or by the sexual implications of Olive Chancellor, reviewers were merely puzzled and bored—by the novel's slow movement and abnormal characters. Mark Twain's remark on the novel is well-known. "I can't stand George Eliot and Hawthorne and those people," he wrote to Howells, ". . . they just bore me to death. And as for *The Bostonians*, I would rather be damned to John Bunyan's heaven than read that."[4] Twain's attitude toward

James's fiction, that it was too minutely and wearisomely psychological, coincided only too closely with that of the American reading public, which rejected both *The Bostonians* and James. The publication of *The Bostonians* marks the point at which James lost his American audience.

The Bostonians was revised only once (very slightly), from the serial to the book version of 1886; and it was not included later in the New York Edition. That James omitted it from the edition, however, does not mean that he had come to think poorly of it. The edition was limited to twenty-three volumes, with the prospect of others being added later, and James expected to include *The Bostonians* in one of these; but because of the edition's disappointing sale, the later volumes were canceled. In 1908, James wrote to Howells that he was considering revising *The Bostonians* for the New York Edition. "But it will take, doubtless," he said, "a great deal of artful redoing—and I haven't, now, had the courage or time for anything so formidable."[5] Later, to Edmund Gosse, he explained that inclusion of the unpopular *Bostonians* had been "rather deprecated by the publishers . . . and there were reasons for which I wanted to wait: we always meant that the work should eventually come in. . . . Revision of it loomed particularly formidable and time-consuming . . . and as other things were more pressing . . . I allowed it to stand over—with the best intentions."[6]

While the edition was being prepared, Howells wrote to James that he feared *The Bostonians* might, after all, be left out, which, he said, "would be the greatest blunder and the greatest pity. Do be persuaded that it is . . . one of the greatest books you have written."[7] Few, however, shared Howells's estimate of *The Bostonians*; and after its publication in 1886—apart from its inclusion in Macmillan's collective edition of James's works in 1921–23—it was not reprinted for fifty-nine years. Carl Van Doren's brief assessment in *The American Novel: 1879–1939* is typical of attitudes toward it expressed in literary histories published before the James revival. "It is," Van Doren commented, "too largely a skeleton, without the blood that might have come from heartier sympathies, without the flesh with which James might have been able to round out a 'purely American' tale had he not forgotten so much about American life. He had forgotten, or at least ceased to care greatly about it."[8] Even Joseph Warren Beach, a warm admirer of James's fiction and the most sensitive of his early critics, describes *The Bostonians* as a rather sad failure, a story "dragged on to tiresome lengths."[9] A tradition of dissatisfaction with *The Bostonians* also includes Rebecca West, Pelham Edgar, C. Hartley Grattan, and more recently Peter Buitenhuis, Oscar Cargill, and Leon Edel.

Yet an affirmative tradition also exists, beginning with essays by Lionel Trilling and Irving Howe, establishing the novel after years of neglect, and extended by many other critics. From a position of obscurity, *The Bostonians* has come to be regarded by many of James's critics as a work of major quality, and it has received enlarged attention in the 1970s. F. R. Leavis states the case for the affirmative position without reservation: *"The Bostonians* is a wonderfully rich, intelligent and brilliant book. . . . It could have been written only by James, and it has an overt richness of life such as is not commonly associated with him. It is incomparably witty and completely serious, and it makes the imputed classical status of all but a few of the admired works of Victorian fiction look silly. It is one of James's achieved major classics, and among the works that he devoted to American life it is supreme."[10]

Source and Influence.   The social background of *The Bostonians* is particularly rich, richer than that of any of the previous novels. Much could be written if space permitted on the relation of the novel to the Woman's Movement, to the Spiritualist movement in America, or, indeed, to actual personalities of the time. Anticipations of *The Bostonians* in James's earlier fiction also makes a subject in itself. Literary influences affecting the novel preclude treatment here except in the most condensed form. Dickens's *Martin Chuzzlewit* (1844), if not a verifiable source, creates at least a precedent for *The Bostonians*. American democracy as it is depicted in Dickens's novel is mired in humbug; the land speculation at Eden turns out to be a swindle, but everything else about the country seems dubious too—even the very nature of American life, which makes no allowance for the privacy of the individual. This publicly oriented life, which shoulders aside a concern with privacy or culture, is represented in *Martin Chuzzlewit* in garish newspapers, endless political discussions, and lectures, at one of which "a wiry-faced damsel" discourses on "the rights of women." The satiric deprecation of American democracy in *The Bostonians* has a kinship of a kind with Dickens's in *Martin Chuzzlewit*, but James is more directly indebted to Dickens in some of the comic modes he uses, particularly in the early section, where characters are viewed from the outside, with a comically two-dimensional effect. A quality of Dickensian humor is particularly evident in the gathering of eccentrics at Miss Birdseye's apartment.

A more pervasive influence on *The Bostonians* is French naturalism, which James had been reassessing in the period leading up to his writing of the novel. When he was staying in Paris in 1884, James wrote to Howells of the increased interest he had been taking in the naturalists' work. "I have been seeing something," he remarked, "of Daudet, Goncourt and Zola; and there is nothing more interesting to me now than the effort and experiment of this little group, with its truly infernal intelligence of art, form, manner—its intense artistic life. They do the only kind of work, today, that I respect; and in spite of their ferocious pessimism and their handling of unclean things, they are at least serious and honest."[11] But it was Daudet, a "poetic" naturalist and the gentlest of the group, in whom James had taken a particular interest. One notices that in his essay "William Dean Howells" (1886) what James singles out for praise is "the compendious, descriptive touch, *a la Daudet*."[12] He even criticizes Howells gently in the essay for his increasing tendency to tell his story altogether in conversations. "The author," he remarks, "sometimes forgets to paint, to evoke the conditions and appearances, to build in the subject." This statement is remarkable for the author of *Confidence*, rendered almost wholly in dialogue, and with social background filled in only meagerly; and it shows how much under the influence of pictorial naturalism James had come by the mid 1880s.

The very specific source for *The Bostonians* is recorded in the notebooks in an entry dated April 8, 1883. "Daudet's *Evangéliste*," James writes, "has given me the idea of this thing. If I could only do something with that *pictorial* quality! At any rate, the subject is very national, very typical. I wished to write a very *American* tale, a tale very characteristic of our social conditions, and I asked myself what was the most salient and peculiar point in our social life. The answer was 'the situation of women, the decline of the sentiment of sex, the agitation on their behalf.' "[13] In his "American" novel, James follows Daudet's "pictorial" method to a very striking degree. His characters are always drawn against their representative cultural background and milieu; their gestures, clothes, and apartments constantly express and evoke them. But *The Bostonians* is indebted to Daudet further in James's peculiar conception of Olive and her association with Verena.[14] In *L'Evangéliste* (1883), Madame Autheman is an evangelist leader rather than a feminist, but her morbidity, sexual maladjustment, and sense of mission that derives from her Calvinist background make her a character very similar in type to Olive. Furthermore, Madame Autheman's adoption of an innocent girl, Eline Ebsen, whose nature she will warp in the pursuit of her own single-minded goals, provides the situation that James explores more elaborately in Olive's adoption of Verena as a protégé.

In giving shape to his conception, however, James also drew significantly from American sources. Bayard Taylor's *Hannah Thurston* (1864) is only one of many popular novels written before *The Bostonians* in which Spiritualism and the Woman's Movement appear together, but more than some others it contains a number of patterns that persist in later novels. Set in a small town in central New York State, a region swept by reforming manias, it deals with a naïve girl, the title character, who becomes a kind of stump speaker for women's rights; a charlatan mesmerist, Dyce, who has formerly been a Spiritualist and medium at séances as well as a member of a free-love colony; and a strong-minded hero, Max Woodbury, who is disgusted by the reforming hoaxes he witnesses, and eventually wins Hannah Thurston away from her utopian illusions. At the end, she marries him and blooms into domestic happiness.

The theme and subject matter of Taylor's *Hannah Thurston* were reshaped sixteen years later by a stronger hand. Howells was familiar with *Hannah Thurston* and there is every suggestion that he was conscious of it while writing his own novel *The Undiscovered Country* (1880), in which the situation between hero and heroine resembles the one in the earlier work. But Howells brings something new to the subject, a concern with the way in which his characters reveal or are revealed by their culture. *The Undiscovered Country* opens upon the scene of a séance in Boston, in which Dr. Boynton exhibits his daughter Egeria as a trance medium; and various characters are encountered who share an interest in Spiritualism as one of the new revelations of the age. What one notices about these characters is that they are treated as manifestations of the deterioration of the culture of New England following the Civil War. At one point the Spiritualists hold a picnic on the shore of Walden Pond, and Howells intimates that a connection exists between the Transcendentalists and the postwar "seekers," but with the difference that the earlier generation's noble search for transcendence, even of the physical world, has become the later's drab and anemic chicanery. In this contrast of generations, *The Undiscovered Country* prepares for James's conception of the generational contrast in *The Bostonians.* Furthermore, Howells's conception of his heroine who is won over to the hero at the end creates a pattern that continues on into James's novel.[15] Howells's naive and radiant Egeria, inspired by voices and exhibited in Boston by her mesmerist father, anticipates James's Verena; just as Ford, a crankish outsider to Boston and critic of its shams, anticipates Basil Ransom. In *The Undiscovered Country*, Ford eventually wrests Egeria from delusive influences, and a similar struggle and denouement are witnessed in *The Bostonians.*

But *The Undiscovered Country* is also indebted to the great parent work of New England reform and utopia novels, Hawthorne's *Blithedale Romance*, the influence of which on *The Bos-*

tonians is major.[16] Hawthorne's romance and James's novel are both concerned with reformers and philanthropists in and near Boston in their own periods; in both, a group of high-aiming reformers seek to reorder society, eliminating from it all the errors and injustices of the past, and making it conform to their own ideals. In both cases, the reformers' idealism is revealed as being a form of illusion, a deception of themselves and others; for while claiming to be motivated by altruism, they actually seek power over others. Hawthorne's principal characters in *The Blithedale Romance* have counterparts in James's novel. Hawthorne's innocent Priscilla, the passive object of others's wills, is the romance ancestress of Verena; and Zenobia, the neurotic champion of women's rights who both seeks and finally achieves martyrdom, is ancestral to Olive. When, in *Hawthorne*, James remarks of *The Blithedale Romance* that he would have liked it to concern itself more with a satire of New England reforming types, he was actually seeing into the future. For in *The Bostonians*, it is almost as if James were demonstrating how *The Blithedale Romance* might have been written and "improved" in the new realism.

Characters Without Homes

The boldness with which James takes imaginative possession of Boston in the novel is evident from the opening pages. Here one encounters Olive Chancellor, the most strenuous of James's "American girls" and the most neurotic, a lonely figure in whom the New England moral virus still lives. She is, as it happens, on her way to attend a meeting of "new women" at Miss Birdseye's apartment in South Boston. At this meeting all of the oddities congregate. Miss Birdseye herself, hostess of this occasion, is a peculiar individual who gives the impression of being out of focus. Her cap, for example, seems as if it were falling back off her head, and her gestures are not synchronized with her speech. Her housemate is a woman doctor whose personal attitudes and interest in applied science are of such a masculine nature that Ransom will later find himself about to offer her a cigar. Present also is the noted women's liberationist, Mrs. Farrinder, a large, cold matron with "a pair of folded arms" (24).[17] Across the room, Selah Tarrant, the unwholesome mesmeric healer, displays his long row of "carnivorous teeth" in a broad smile, and exclaims: "I guess we are all solid here" (38).

James's humor in *The Bostonians*, which ranges from the glacially ironic to the natively American and colloquial, takes the form of a satire of democratic manners—the public orientation of individual's private lives. Olive's drawing room, for example, presumably a place of innermost privacy, has the shape of a corridor; and Miss Birdseye's parlor, when chairs are arranged along its sides for the meeting, has the "similitude of an enormous streetcar" (25). All of those present are depicted as having been influenced in their attitudes and natures by public life. Miss Birdseye wears, rather than a dress, a loose black jacket, the pockets of which are stuffed with her political correspondence; and Mrs. Farrinder is "a mixture of the American matron and the public character" (24). Dr. Tarrant's nature is pitched "in the key of public life" (62), and he gestures with his hands "as if he were being photographed in postures" (86). Because of the public definition Miss Birdseye and the members of her circle have been given, a question is raised as to their inner lives. Many are said to be "formless," to have no "figure," no personal outline.

In *The American Scene*, written much later in his life, James again examines American social reality in relation to "the sense of place," and passages in it are relevant to *The Bostonians*. Early in the book, James refers the question of manners to the American home. "That, precisely," he remarks, "appeared to be the answer to the question of manners: the fact that in such conditions there couldn't *be* any manners to speak of; that the basis of privacy was somehow wanting for them; and that nothing, accordingly, no image, no presumption of constituted relations, possibilities, amenities, in the social, the domestic order, was inwardly projected. It was as if the projection had all been ... completely outward."[18] The home, as the basis of privacy and ultimately of all manners, enters into *The Bostonians* at many points. Olive has a refined home on Charles Street, but she has made it the setting of stern duties rather than of relaxed pleasures; it becomes the scene of a bookish loneliness and torment. Miss Birdseye may have an apartment, but it cannot properly be called a home, since it is sometimes the setting of political meetings but never of purely personal enjoyment. Her quarters consist of a parlor described variously as "bald," "barren," and "empty"; Olive has to kill the nerve of her aesthetic susceptibilities in order to visit it. Comparing her circumstances with the older woman's midway in the novel, she reflects that Miss Birdseye "had only a bare, vulgar room, with a hideous flowered carpet (it looked like a dentist's), a cold furnace, the evening paper, and Doctor Prance" (154).

In New York, Ransom knows almost no one, and lives in "two shabby rooms" of a decayed Second Avenue building, the shutters of which are "limp and at variance with each other" (157). His window view looks out, across an unpaved street containing ruts a foot deep, at a row of ugly tenements. Toward the corner, at the end of a "truncated vista," the view takes in "the fantastic skeleton of the Elevated Railway, overhanging the transverse street, which it darkened and smothered with the immeasurable spinal column and myriad clutching paws of an antediluvian monster" (158). This description suggests claustrophobia and incoherence rather than the amenities and stabilizing influences that might be found in a home.

But the Tarrants' house in Cambridge is also depressing. A footway from the unpaved road before it is overlaid with planks which, James remarks, "were embedded in ice or liquid thaw, according to the momentary mood of the weather, and the advancing pedestrian traversed them in the attitude, and with a good deal of suspense, of a rope-dancer" (98). The prospect within is equally bleak, since the parlor, which reeks of kerosene, is practically empty. The only objects in it that are noted are a wooden chair that creeks when someone sits in it and a stand with a japanned tray containing Dr. Tarrant's professional cards, denominating him a mesmeric healer. The Tarrants' dwelling gives an almost poignant irony to Mrs. Tarrant's remarking to people, on several occasions, that she would be happy to see them in her home—unaware, as she obviously is, of what a home signifies or what the forms of social intercourse are.

The Function of Landscape

The characters' attitudes have been affected, too, by surroundings that extend beyond the home itself; and an unusual amount of attention has been given to physical landscapes. The settings of the novel are chiefly urban, and the characters are typically seen against the background of their urban milieu. Olive's window view of the Charles River as it is described at the opening reveals the environmental background that has influenced her character. In this window view at sunset "the afternoon sun slants redly, from an horizon indented at empty intervals with wooden spires, the masts of lonely boats, the chimneys of dirty 'works,' over a brackish expanse of anomalous character, which is too big for a river and too small for a bay. . . . in the gathered dusk little was left of [the view] save a cold yellow streak in the west, a gleam of brown water" (12). In this impression, in a way traditional with the literary naturalists, James uses dim light and dingy yellows and browns to evoke a feeling of dreariness. The water is "brackish," and several adjectives are especially revealing—"odd," "lonely," and "empty." Elements in the landscape also clash; the body of water itself is "anomalous," being neither river nor bay, and ultimately the picture fails to "compose."

The view from Olive's window is emphasized again when Verena comes to stay with Olive during a Boston winter, and the passage describing it is so revealing that it deserves to be quoted in full:

The western windows of Olive's drawing-room, looking over the water, took in the red sunsets of winter; the long, low bridge that crawled, on its staggering posts, across the Charles; the casual patches of ice and snow; the desolate suburban horizons, peeled and made bald by the rigour of the season; the general hard, cold void of the prospect; the extrusion, at Charlestown, at Cambridge, of a few chimneys and steeples, straight, sordid tubes of factories and engine-shops, or spare, heavenward finger of the New England meeting-house. There was something inexorable in the poverty of the scene, shameful in the meanness of its details, which gave a collective impression of boards and tin and frozen earth, sheds and rotting pipes, railway lines striding flat across a thoroughfare of puddles and tracks of the humbler, universal horse-car, traversing obliquely this path of danger; loose fences, vacant lots, mounds of refuse, yards bestrewn with iron pipes, telegraph poles, and bare wooden backs of places . . . as the afternoon closed, the ugly picture was tinted with a clear, cold rosiness. (149)

In this later view, the scene has become immeasurably more depressing. It suggests an industrial society at a point of near breakdown. Its chief impression is one of ugliness and inertia, of mud and ice, of stymied energy.

This impression of urban blight in New England is duplicated in other scenes laid in New York. In the description of Ransom's neighborhood, tenements built not long before have already become delapidated, unpaved streets contain huge puddles of "stagnant mud," sidewalk flagstones are "dislocated," "disjointed" elevated railways command and darken the view. At one point only, before the late scene set on Cape Cod, is there any intermission from such oppressiveness, when Ransom and Verena visit Central Park. There they come for a moment into a prospect, however imperfect, of sunlight and nature, have a sense of "air and space." When they leave the park and enter onto Sixth Avenue, however, the aerial perspective is immediately lost as tall commercial buildings block out the light. These landscapes speak for the industrial age following the Civil War that has brought merely an increasing loneliness and isolation, a dreary fragmentation of vision.

The Cast of Characters

The sense of decay and aberrancy that accrues in the novel is relevant to James's depiction of the reformers. A stigma attaches to them, in the first place, through their association, even if unwil-

lingly, with Dr. Tarrant. Although professing a high-minded disinterestedness, he is always alert to self-advancement of some
kind, whether through attention in the press or coin in his pocket.
His exploitation of his daughter is a form of self-promotion, one
that he hopes will result, to use his own word, in "receipts." So consummate a humbug he is that even in the privacy of his home he
never lets his mask slip, addressing his wife at the dinner table
in the same tone of lofty aims that he employs in public, although
she has been thoroughly exposed to his shams and has taken part
in some of them. In Mrs. Tarrant, indeed, one sees the inexorable
wearing away of ideals to the point where they can no longer be
clearly remembered. The daughter of Abraham Greenstreet, the
abolitionist famous for his strong moral sense, Mrs. Tarrant has
since shuffled and wheeled with her husband in the course of a
migratory life, involving, among other things, the practice of
fraudulent séances; and by the time the novel opens, she has but
one forlorn ambition left, to rise somehow out of the swamp of
the humanitary bohemia into which she has sunk to her chin.

Miss Birdseye is the most truly disinterested of the reformers
and has the purest integrity, but even so it is obvious that there
is something wrong with her. Her spectacles, in which the moral
history of Boston is said to be reflected, are "undiscriminating," and
her eyesight is "weak." She has supported indigent artists, believing in their genius, but has no understanding of the fine arts, and
has expended her energies in behalf of almost any cause whatever.
In Miss Birdseye, one sees the very tendencies of democracy—its
formlessness and attraction to whatever is most current or most
loudly cried up. But she has also been revealed by her Transcendental origins. Olive reflects that it "was the perennial freshness of
Miss Birdseye's faith that had such a contagion for these modern
maidens, the unquenched flame of her transcendentalism, the simplicity of vision, the way in which . . . the only thing that was still
actual for her was the elevation of the species by the reading of
Emerson" (153). Elsewhere, James wrote of the curiously disembodied quality of Emerson's mind, his impartiality and "passion-
lessness." He had, James remarked, "no personal, just as he had

almost no physical wants."[19] Miss Birdseye has been given a similar Transcendental abstractness, a moral perception of life rather than a sharply individualized or deeply personal one. Her clothes fit her, revealingly, "as if she had worn them for many years and was even now imperfectly acquainted with them" (180). Miss Birdseye is treated with increasing tenderness as the novel progresses, and her death at Marmion, on Cape Cod, forms one of the most poignant episodes of the work. But even in this scene, the reader does not forget her eighty years of illusion; the scene is poignant partly because of the sense one has that Miss Birdseye has never really had a "life."

It is against Miss Birdseye's genuine disinterestedness that Olive and the others of the later generation are measured. Olive is odd and aberrant, but aberration attaches to the others too. Mrs. Luna's fervid sexuality forms a distinct contrast to her sister's sexual coldness, but she is like Olive in that she, too, has no sense of proportion. She lacks restraint, as James implies when he writes of her, in great comic image, that her "tight bodice seemed to crack with vivacity" (3). Mrs. Luna throws herself at Ransom almost as soon as she meets him, beseiges him with invitations to her home in New York, and when there proposes to "drive him in the Park at unnatural hours" (165). When he declines to accompany her on the pretext of business, she exclaims: "Oh, a plague on your business! I am sick of that word—one hears of nothing else in America. There are ways of getting on without business, if you will only take them!" (165). Offering the bribe of her financial security, she attempts to entrap the impoverished Ransom into matrimony.

Mrs. Luna's femininity becomes a form of assault upon men, and there is in it a form of assertiveness traditionally associated with masculinity. That such commingling of masculine and feminine elements in Mrs. Luna's sexuality is cultural in nature is borne out by James's Bostonian men, who are shown as being effeminized. Amariah Farrinder is a mute appendage to his overpowering wife, and follows meekly behind her on each occasion he appears; Henry Burrage, like Ned Rosier in *The Portrait of a Lady*, decorates his mantel with Spanish altar cloths, and is a dilettante whose mother courts Verena for him; and Pardon, who uses mincing expressions like "mercy on us," is only too willing to "serve" the ladies in the press. *The Bostonians* depicts a society in which traditional forms, including even sexual identity itself, have entered a phase of breakdown.

Basil Ransom is the only really masculine character in the novel, and the reader is apt to feel some sympathy for him, in the earlier part at least, as Olive's opponent and a beleaguered outsider; but as a character he is not an entirely successful conception. He has been given a passionate nature and Mississippian virility, but the opening description emphasizes his Southern associations to the point of caricature. His eyes, for example, have a "smouldering fire" (2), and his discourse is "pervaded by something sultry and vast, something almost African in its rich basking tone, something that suggested the teeming expanse of the cotton-field" (2). James's characterization of Ransom depends to a large degree on the stereotype of the Southerner in popular novels of the Reconstruction period, the Southerner as he had come to be eroticized in the imagination of the North. As a Southerner, he lacks fullness of specification, and the ruined plantation he is supposed to have left behind in Mississippi seems factitious. Even considered more generally, he is more of an outline than a delineated character. Admitting as much himself in a letter of 1885 to John Hay, James wrote that Ransom "is made up of wandering airs and chance impressions, and I fear that as the story goes on he doesn't become as solid as he ought to be. He remains a rather vague and artificial creation, and so far as he looks at all real, is only *fait de chic*."[20]

James's strongest characters in the novel are women. Miss Birdseye is drawn with a richly individualized humanity, and she is a superb creation, a character treated with tenderness even when one laughs at her, as one does when Ransom tells her that women have no business to be reasonable, and she replies: "Do you regard us, then, simply as lovely baubles?" (183). Dr. Prance is another of James's triumphs in the work, a New England woman comically dry and limited in her view of life who is yet treated by Ransom with an old-fashioned chivalry. Mrs. Luna's existence is circumscribed by drawing rooms, like those of other women in James's earlier novels, but she has a sharp pointedness and particularity. It is typical of her that, on her second meeting with Ransom, when he tells her that he does not understand a woman like Olive, she should attempt to appropriate him, remarking archly: "Come away with me, and I'll explain her as we go" (81); and that, deserted by Ransom at Mrs. Burrage's gathering, she should be observed "still seated on her sofa—alone in the lamplit desert—with her eyes making, across the empty space, little vindictive points" (222). Although a subordinate character, Mrs. Burrage is authoritatively portrayed. Her *tête-à-tête* with Olive in chapter thirty-two, a scene in which the Boston spinster is made to confront the New York matron in the full force of her subtlety and intelligence, is handled with the suave understanding of women that distinguishes James as a novelist of manners.

The Portrait of Olive Chancellor

But the great character in *The Bostonians* is Olive. *The Europeans* prepares for her in some respects, since like the Wentworths her New England conscience has made her old before she has ever been young. As Mr. Wentworth looks as if he were undergoing martyrdom "by freezing," Olive presents "a certain appearance of feeling cold" (15); and as a light in his face might have "flashed back from an iceberg," Olive's eyes make Ransom think of "the glitter of green ice" (15). Mr. Wentworth receives Eugenia as a duty rather than a pleasure, and Olive always has in mind "not a pleasure, but a duty" (14).

Yet Olive also evolves from James's earlier studies of women who are self-deceived—including Isabel Archer in *The Portrait of a Lady*. It is exactly the Puritan-Transcendental heritage Isabel and Olive both embrace that estranges them from life; Isabel's sense of mission is alluded to repeatedly, and it is a distinctively New England sense of mission that impels Olive. Olive's agitated New England conscience gives her no ease of relation to life. Her house in Back Bay becomes a "headquarters," from which she wages her campaigns, a place where the great reforming names of the past, like that of Eliza P. Moseley, are mentioned reverently. Eliza P. Moseley does not appear in the work, but she is referred to several times, and at one point is made to suggest an actual person—Harriet Beecher Stowe, author of *Uncle Tom's Cabin* (in which the runaway slave girl, Eliza, is a character). Hearing her fulsomely praised, Ransom exclaims that she had been "the cause of the biggest war of which history preserves the record" (77)—words that paraphrase the greeting of President Lincoln to Mrs. Stowe when she was taken to call on him at the White House: "So this is the little lady who made this big war." In *Uncle Tom's Cabin*, the salvationist energies of the Puritan imagination have been diverted to polemical reform, have entered the arena of crusading politics; and the Puritan imagination survives in Olive, a morbid reformer.

Olive has a kinship not only with the Puritans but also with the Transcendentalists, with their moral abstractness, quest for lonely sublimity, and concern with self-culture. Margaret Fuller had been a particular votary among the Transcendentalists of self-culture (it was typical of her that she had read immensely in Goethe), and she is a silent presence in the background of Olive, who has something of her bookishness and ardent concern with intellectual ennoblement. Like the Transcendentalists, Olive frequents the Tremont Temple, where she is enraptured by the music of Beethoven—who had been to Emerson's generation in music what Goethe had been in literature. In thunder, Beethoven had announced the greatness of the individual's striving, the democratic vision, the imminent overthrow of injustice and regeneration of the world. It is under the Olympian bust of Beethoven that Olive "worships."

Olive's heroic mode of perception, belonging more to a past age than to her own, makes her the victim of continual self-deception. Her habits of mind often reveal her involvement in a psychological juggle in which black becomes white. She forbids herself to be "personal," so that when she finds herself detesting Dr. Tarrant she has to assure herself that she dislikes him only "as a type." Through a similar process of rationalizing away what she does not want to face, she affirms that she dislikes men only "as a class." In embracing democracy as her ideal, she has to tell herself fables, that only very obscure people, toilers and spinners, are free from the taint of vulgarity. She rides the horse-car to share the lot of the less privileged, but the experience always lacerates her taste. The most poignant thing about her is that she continually lacerates, or crucifies, her taste for the sake of her theories. It seems a crucifixion of her taste, for example, that she should choose to stay at a New Jerusalem boardinghouse while in New York, a haven for utopian reformers having a "hot, faded" parlor with a rug "representing a Newfoundland dog saving a child from drowning" (237).

When Olive first appears, James says of her that her "white skin had a singular look of being drawn tightly across her face" (15), which gives her face a masklike effect, and implies a difference that exists between her formal avowals and her inner necessities. She urges her "cause" upon Verena as a heavenly mission; and during the winter Verena spends with her they are pictured in "the early darkness, pacing quietly side by side, in their winter robes, like women consecrated to some holy office" (132). Yet what lies behind Olive's vision of feminine ennoblement is "silent rage." The darker energies in Olive are evoked at times as being of some demonic kind. She is seen at the beginning with her eyes cast fixedly on the floor, as if there had been a spell upon her" (7), and thereafter the vocabulary of enchantments and unnatural spells is employed repeatedly. At one point, Olive is said to have Verena "under the charm" (143); and in the early scene at the Tarrants' cottage, she seizes an opportunity "to take a more complete possession of the girl" (111). Outside, in the wintry night, having the aura of a cold, sharp cruelty, she enfolds Verena within her cloak and asks her to promise never to marry, to sacrifice—her life.

The romance element of their association is intensified further by Verena's having been made remarkably innocent. She is described as a "spotless, consecrated maiden" (255), and a "charming, blooming simple creature, all youth and grace and innocence" (70).

At times she gives the strong suggestion of a naively pure heroine of fairy tale. When her mother coaches her about the advantages of an intimacy with Olive, Verena listens "as she would have listened to any other fairy tale" (59). It is "still part of the fairy tale" (59) when she is sent off for the first time to visit Olive at her home. It is like a fairy tale that she should be taken up by Olive, and yet be held by her under a sinister duress; that she should be too simple to perceive the danger in which she is placed; that Ransom should appear as a rescuing knight, and that knight and witch should contend for her soul; that, at the Boston Music Hall, freed at last from Olive's hold over her, she should flee with Ransom into the night.

It is part of the romance conception of Olive that she should be felt by the reader as a character who has made some sort of evil compact, as with the devil, and that she should be the fateful temptress of another. Early in the novel, Olive inspires Verena with a lofty vision that derives from her own thirst for knowledge, absolute intellect. "Olive had taken her up," James remarks, "in the literal sense of the phrase, like a bird of the air, had spread an extraordinary pair of wings, and carried her through the dizzying void of space. Verena liked it, for the most part; liked to shoot upward without an effort of her own and look down upon all creation, upon all history, from such a height" (66). This passage is similar to the one in *Paradise Lost* in which the angel Michael reveals the earth through all time and history to Adam. The passage had been intimated earlier in *The Portrait of a Lady* when, in the grip of intellectual pride, Isabel chooses to marry Osmond; and it was followed by the scene of her "fall." Olive, too, is guilty of overreaching pride, and her pride is later punished. Among the many things that Olive does not understand is that her attraction to the lovely, young Verena has not only a very personal but even a sexual basis. James's handling of Olive's unconscious lesbianism is extremely suave, but everything in the novel points to it and James's intention is clear. Olive has deceived herself even as to the most rudimentary facts of her nature. She acknowledges only a heavenly mission, great abstractions that are to lead in time to

great deeds; but eventually she is made to confront the discrepancy
between her strenuous imaginings and the simple nature of things.

Her recognition occurs at Marmion, when Ransom arrives to
lay claim to Verena, and their romance blooms with the blooming
of nature around them. Jilted, in effect, as Verena spends an entire
afternoon with Ransom, on a sailboat on the bay, after she had
promised Olive never to see him again, Olive walks alone by the
water and as it comes over her that her imaginings have never
been based in reality she emits a long, low wail of pain. "The sense
of regret for her baffled calculations," James writes, "burned
within her like a fire, and the splendour of the vision over which the
curtain of mourning now was dropped brought to her eyes slow,
silent tears that came one by one, neither easing her nerves nor
lightening her load of pain" (345). She can think now only of "the
misery of such a fall after such a flight" (345). Olive's "fall,"
from her paradise of lofty imaginings, is accompanied, moreover,
by the motif of New England's fall. The decline of the old New
England towns, prosperous a generation before, the death of Miss
Birdseye, a monument to the earlier age, insinuate the more general theme of the fall of heroic illusion.

Olive's terrible illusion is intimated, moreover, by the specific
literature she reads. When Verena first goes to see her, their
conversation turns to Goethe. Olive asks Verena: "Do you understand German? Do you know 'Faust'?" (72); and after Verena
replies that she wants "to know everything," Olive pants: "we
will study everything" (73). Olive then asks her if she knows the
meaning of the words from *Faust: "Entsagen sollst du, sollst
entsagen!"* (72), which she renders as "Thou shalt renounce, re-
frain, abstain" (73). What Olive is asking of the girl is a renunciation of life itself. The implications of *"entsagen"* become even
more sinister when one remembers what *"entsagen"* meant to
Goethe—a purgatorial suffering leading to a higher state of soul
purity. What Olive enjoins upon Verena here is heroic suffering.

Olive's fate is so harsh that nothing comparable to it exists in
James's earlier novels. More characteristically, his villains are
punished by having to confront their own powerlessness and

negativity. Madame Merle is punished more than some others, for in addition to having to make such a recognition, she returns to America, where, without the support of social forms and manners, her life will essentially be extinguished. But Olive is punished with deep and lasting torment. What her life will be like after the Music Hall debacle can be imagined because the reader is already conscious of her "fearful power of suffering" (247); and Verena predicts Olive's future when she thinks of the "dreadful years" in which she "would be incurably lonely and eternally humiliated" (325). It is part of the boldness of James's conception of Olive that he should inflict such an unprecedently terrible fate upon her; and there is an intimation in the novel that the role Olive enacts is analogous to that of Faust. Allusions to *Faust* of various kinds appear in the novel (including references to witches on the Brocken at the beginning and a grinning Mephistopheles at the end), together with hints of diabolic possession. Olive is like Faust in her isolation and compulsion to dominate life through will and intellect. Faust's is the supreme act of intellectual pride, and his pride in self and restless torment are implied in Olive. Her going out at the end to face the howling mob at the Music Hall, and what will follow for her, is a kind of Faustian damnation, a damnation in Boston.

In his searching essay on *The Bostonians*, Graham Burns has argued that James's study of Olive "takes on a singularity and a pathological aspect which removes it from the symptomatic and cultural."[21] She is too special a case, it seems to him, to be representative of her environment. But surely Olive's "case" is relevant to New England. She is, strictly speaking, no more typical of Back Bay than Captain Ahab is typical of Nantucket; but in the very extremity of her case, she reveals the inner stresses and limitations of her culture—its righteous moral sense that may, if carried beyond a certain point, become horrifyingly inhuman or yield to a self-devouring isolation and torment. Olive dramatizes James's brief against the New England moral imagination more powerfully than any more nearly normal character could ever have done.

The Portrait of Basil Ransom

At the end, with the overthrow of Olive at the Music Hall, the reader is apt to feel that Verena's future contains potentialities for self-realization that it had not before. Yet the fairy-tale ending is suddenly made suspect by the final view of Verena in tears, "not the last she was destined to shed" (378), and the realization that her destination is Ransom's dismal dwelling on Second Avenue. Lyall Powers has explained the conclusion by commenting that "all the natural impulse of the novel is directed toward the 'happy-ending' James gives it,"[22] and that the qualification of tears does not cancel out James's optimistic intention. But Powers's impression of a genial ending has been disputed by other critics of the work, including Martha Banta and Susan Wolstenholme, who find the ending bleakly pessimistic. A careful reading of the novel not only supports this view, but makes it seem practically irrefutable. What occurs at the end is that Verena passes from the control of one oppressor to that of another.

If Olive's reading of Goethe provides a clue to her psychology, Ransom's reading of Carlyle provides a clue to his. What can be noticed about Ransom at the beginning is that he possesses a kind of power lust. He is said to have "an immense desire for success" (13), "a bigger stomach than all the culture of Charles Street could fill" (14)—an image of ambition that seems devouring. His attitude toward women, that they are inferior to men, and should be "gracious and grateful" (163), belongs to a plantation psychology of master and slave, of power relationships. Although he advocates "privacy" as an ultimate ideal, his actual associations are with public life. "He had always had a desire," James writes, "for public life; to cause one's ideas to be embodied in national conduct seemed to him the highest form of human enjoyment" (160). He is even described physically as belonging to the public sector of life, his head being the kind to be seen "above the level of a crowd, on some . . . political platform, or even on a bronze medal" (2). Like Olive, Ransom will politicize the home to which he takes Verena, using it as a substitute for the outward power he craves but does not have, and regarding his subjugation of her in terms of the highest-minded idealism.

Ironically perhaps, the character with whom Ransom has most in common is Olive. As has been noted earlier, characters placed in opposition in James's novels often turn out to be very much like one another. Dr. Sloper and Morris Townsend, although locked in contention as adversaries, have similar natures and a similar desire to control Catherine; and even Isabel Archer and Gilbert Osmond turn out to have more in common than they might at first seem to have, in their mutually abstract and absolute sense of self. Ransom and Olive are starkly contrasted as Southerner of the deepest dye and Northerner of the most tenacious imprint, as royalist with smouldering eyes and Puritan with eyes of ice. Yet both are ideologues, with a religious element to their thinking. Olive estranges herself from normative human relationships to find holy purification in suffering; and Ransom finds spiritual aggrandizement, even if at the loss of his humanity, by imposing his will upon his foes. The moment of exultation for Olive and Ransom occurs at exactly the same time, in the final moments of the novel at the Boston Music Hall.

The ability of Olive and Ransom to see themselves realistically is curtailed by their sense of mission. Olive envisions herself leading a crusade that will culminate in triumph at some time in the future; and Ransom dreams of reinstating the past. Olive's easily shattered nerves, headaches, and tears hardly qualify her for a crusading role; and Ransom is too impractical to impose himself on the world, and cannot, in fact, succeed even as a lawyer of a small pattern. Yet in their overworked imaginations, and perhaps even because they sense their helplessness, they envision themselves playing grandiose roles. Ransom has "visions of greatness" that he has temporarily had to stifle, quixotic dreams of "his earthly destiny" (158). Being wholly without power, his sense of mission is directed toward wresting Verena from Olive, which is the only form of power that is available to him. He repeatedly thinks of himself as "saving" her, even feels that she is "praying to be rescued, to be saved" (362) by him. Yet Olive thinks of Verena in exactly the same way, wishes to "rescue the girl from the danger of vulgar exploitation" (70)—from the Tarrants, and from a series of men, most particularly Ransom. With their sense of mission, they do not recognize the selfish uses they themselves make of Verena, and are largely unable to see her apart from what they project of their own inner drives upon her.

The love motif at Marmion is persuasive but also misleading, for Ransom's "love" is undercut by the implication that it is, after all, a crude form of coercion. James remarks of Verena that "it was in her nature to be easily submissive, to like being over-borne" (278); and it is said specifically that she yields to Olive because of her stronger will. Later, however, when Ransom has the upper hand, Verena finds herself "yielding to a will which she felt to be stronger even than Olive's" (278); and in the vocabulary associated with Olive, he is said "to take possession of Verena" (23) and to cast a "spell" over her. By the Music Hall scene, there is no longer any semblance of benevolence in Ransom's attitude. James writes that however Verena "might turn and twist in his grasp he held her fast" (338). The cruelty implied in the image is borne out in his imposing terms of total and uncon-ditional defeat upon Olive. His wresting of Verena from her publicly will, it seems to him, "symbolize his victory" (330), and it is implied that this victory is a form of revenge of South over North, a retaliation for the humiliation and unconditional defeat imposed upon his native region.

As Ransom leaves the Music Hall with Verena, he throws a cloak over her "to conceal her face and her identity" (377), and in doing so repeats the gesture of Olive, who had enfolded Verena in her cloak as she took possession of her in Cambridge. Such concealment of her identity indicates her future with Ransom, and its implications are the more important when one considers what Verena represents. She is described as having the "consummate innocence of the American girl" (104), and as being "a flower of the great Democracy" (94); she comes to suggest spiritual beauty appearing in a democracy, even in the humblest or most unlikely places. "You stand apart," Ransom tells her, "you are unique, extraordinary; you constitute a category by yourself. In you the elements have become mixed in a manner so felicitous that I regard you as quite incorruptible. I don't know where you come from nor how you come to be what you are, but you are outside and above all vulgarizing influences" (285). Yet Verena has been vulgarized by almost everyone around her, and as the wife of Ransom, who has previously affirmed that were she to speak he would find a way to strike her dumb, she will suffer yet further distortion of identity.

Conclusion

In James's envisioning of democracy in *The Bostonians*, the characters' potentialities for self-realization are so circumscribed that Ransom and Verena themselves are unable to qualify for hero and heroine roles. Their environment does not permit such full development, since the self-concern and self-assertion which it embodies can lead only to strife and the deformation of personality.

The brief scene at Memorial Hall, which forms an intermission in the strife of the novel, evokes a set of values at variance with those of the culture. The memorial to the Civil War dead speaks not of narrow animosities but of generous impulse and large perspectives—of duty, honor, and self-sacrifice. It is not heroically magnified, but conforms to a human scale and speaks to what might be called the "soul." The memory it evokes for Ransom arches "over friends as well as enemies, the victims of defeat as well as the sons of triumph" (205). This reminder of the "common doom," the universal human circumstance, restores for a moment a sense of proportion, of the sacredness of the individual's relation to others and to the life of mankind. In one of her speeches, Verena speaks of women as the "heart" of humanity, but in the novel women as much as men have abdicated "heart," or a reverential sense of life, for "head"—intellectualized consciousness and self-assertion.

The Bostonians marks a dividing point in James's career in many respects. Conspicuously, it was the last novel James completed to be set on American soil. But it indicates a dividing point also in its comprehensive cultural perspective, of a kind found nowhere else in the previous novels; this enlarged perspective shows James at a point of summation in regard to his homeland. Despite the gustiness and obvious relish of the satire in the first third of the novel, the work ends with a sense of James's alienation from American life in the 1880s. The death of both of his parents shortly before *The Bostonians* was written no doubt contributed to the novel's mood, in which one has the impression that James's last remaining ties with his native land are now gone. The unusual importance given in the work to the home, the home that for Americans hardly exists, seems relevant to the loss of his own home after his parents' death; and never before in James's novels has the sense of alienation in America been registered so sharply.

Curiously, just as James summed up his homeland, his homeland reached its summation of him as a novelist it need no longer read. The conflict between James and his American audience had been apparent earlier in James's attitudes toward New England in *The Europeans* and *Hawthorne*, which picture a society of stifling narrowness; and in the hostility of the attacks on James in reviews of those books. But *The Bostonians* marks the point of departure between author and audience. Smugly, the Colonel Higginsons found *The Bostonians* unworthy even of serious consideration, and in doing so they ruled the reflective novel out of bounds to American art. Not until two decades later did James revisit his homeland, a visit that occasioned his brilliant travel book *The American Scene*, in which one has the impression of James as a visitor from a more highly evolved planet attempting to comprehend American social reality. What happened to James in the course of his later career as a novelist abroad is reflected in the sense of alienation one finds in *The American Scene*, which magnifies that in *The Bostonians* to the hundredth power.

Chapter Nine

Conclusion

When James began publishing at the end of the Civil War no tradition of realism as yet existed in America. The burden of establishing such a tradition fell upon James and his contemporaries, particularly Mark Twain and Howells, who, in their different ways, began to define the nature of American life in a framework of realistic observation. But the three started out with different sets of commitments, and of these James's were the most complicated by his travel abroad and absorption of the culture and art of Europe. It was by a European standard that he tended to regard America in his earliest stories, and this habit of comparative appraisal persists throughout his career. In *The Bostonians*, James employs some of the techniques of French naturalism, but Europe is important to the novel more deeply in the cultural attitudes he brings to it. Although *The Bostonians* is set entirely in America, Europe is still present in it, even if unnamed, in the alternative values that are implied—Europe's history and art, standards and forms, that make for a civilized and conscious life.

In his own time James was sometimes perceived as a writer whose American nationality was an accident of birth, and whose allegiances were wholly European. But it would be more accurate to see in him a long and unresolved conflict between the legacy bequeathed to him by his native land and family, and the European heritage he embraced. Such a divided heritage can be illustrated even in the influences affecting his fiction. Of the European influences that touched him profoundly that of Turgenev is the most demonstrable, and in his own time James was often compared to him. In Turgenev's realism, the author virtually disappears; he ceases to intrude onto the narration, to explain his characters to the reader, or even to provide an explanation at the end as to what the experience portrayed may mean. The reader himself, in this "dramatic novel," is forced to do the work of understanding, just as he might as a participant in actual experience. Turgenev, in this way, contributed to James's conception of the novel. But he affected James in other ways as well. His concern with form and "architecture"—his selection of a limited number of characters, placed in patterns of parallelism and contrast, and kept in sharp focus by a moral idea—is reflected in the structure of James's works. Turgenev is particularly evident in the background of *Roderick Hudson* and *The American*, but in James's use of character parallels and oppositions, and "open" but enigmatic endings, he never really disappears.

One might say that James learned his art abroad, except that it was an American art, and in many ways different from Turgenev's. Nowhere in Turgenev, for example, does one encounter the mythic imagination found in James. Turgenev's characters frequently meet with frustration or become moral failures; but in James, frustration and failure characteristically suggest the imagination of cultural fable or morality, and have quasi-Christian overtones. A Turgenev hero fails, but a Jamesian hero "falls." Although belonging to psychological realism, the novels continually ally themselves with the moral themes and large, abstracting contours of the American prose romance of the generation before James's own. Hawthorne, in particular, is the real father figure to James. Certain of James's novels, such as *Roderick Hudson* and *The Bostonians*, are particularly indebted to Hawthorne, but his influence is pervasive. Hawthorne's persistent theme of "heart" violated by "head" recurs all through James's fiction, as may be seen in a procession of characters in the earlier novels, from Rowland Mallet to Olive Chancellor. James's approach to the novel as a psychological investigator concerned with the sharp intensities of inner experience,

and the fable dimension beneath the surface of this realism, all
show James's derivation from a native tradition in fiction.

Such drawing upon different traditions at once, American as
well as European, is part of a pattern of duality in James that
can be noticed in many other ways. The international theme, which
occupies the foreground of the earlier novels, appropriates cultures
both native and transatlantic; James's equation necessarily requires
both. Characteristically, his American questors go abroad in order
to achieve self-realization, to discover themselves, or to test their
assumptions in the context of the great world. Roderick Hudson
is typical of these early questors, and of the values they espouse—
freedom, the individual, self-fulfillment. In the New England
village of Northampton, he is "safe," but his life is cramped, and
the means it affords him for self-expression is extremely limited.
His life in Italy, however, merely brings out his latent destructive
tendencies; the grandeur and sublimity to which he is dedicated
become the egotistic obsession that interferes with his realization
of a stable identity. His freedom becomes chaos, his nobility ig-
nobility, his lust for life a longing for death. One of the questions
Roderick Hudson asks is whether Roderick might better have remained in America, which would not have deprived him, as Italy
does, of his sense of proportion. But Europe in the novel is presented as being neither wholly good nor bad, and James's America
is viewed with the same ambivalence. The opposing cultures, rather,
provide context for the drama of perception.

In *The American*, Christopher Newman is preeminently an
American democrat, a believer in endless self-expansion; the idea
of closure is abhorrent to him. Yet in Europe he is "closed out"
by the Bellegardes; a check is delivered to his aspirations, even
to his sense of himself. On the surface it might appear that Newman is a "good" American abused by a French aristocracy not
only mean and self-serving but actually evil, flagrantly immoral.
His declining to retaliate upon the Bellegardes at the end might
be seen as the victory of the American democrat's generous spirit
over the decadent institutionalized life of the old world. Upon
reflection, however, one recognizes that the victory is the old

world's, which has chastened Newman's consciousness, and introduced him to the inner life. Newman's abnegation of self at the end is a "correction" of his exaggerated American sense of life as being wholly outward, the will limitless, the self absolute. In *The American*, America and Europe come to represent ideas, which have a relative or corrective relationship to each other.

In *The Europeans*, James brings the international theme home, contrasting a sharply particularized New England with a Europe that is indicated largely through implication. The New England milieu is fixed and immutable, but Europe is both real and somewhat dreamlike, containing possibilities for the individual to realize his nature that are left open. The Wentworths stay at home, but Felix and Eugenia travel, and their traveling intimates the play of imagination that New England prohibits. But, once again, the cultural contrast is relative. The pale decency of the Wentworths sometimes occasions laughter, but both Felix and Eugenia are less than what they might be. Eugenia, in particular, is suspect: mercenary as well as charming, soiled as well as attractive. Her leaving at the end depletes New England of what small amount of life it has been able to sustain; but her going back to Silberstadt-Schreckenstein, the associations of which are the opposite of innocent, is a return to a setting that had oppressed and disillusioned her in the first place.

But the international theme achieves its largest orchestration, among the earlier novels, in *The Portrait of a Lady*. Most of the novel's characters are Americans who have lived abroad; Osmond and his sister, the Countess Gemini, are of partly American origin but have been expatriated for so long and to such a degree that they have come to represent Europe much more than America; and the same is true of Madame Merle, whose very "shape" and all of whose values bear the imprint of European forms and attitudes. They have all achieved the finish of a high civilization, but they have also lost their innocence. Europe has improved them, but it has also made them worse, disturbed their values. Osmond's European absorption with art has affected him so profoundly that his judgments are aesthetic rather than moral, and he consequently no longer has a sense of reality. Isabel, on the other hand, embodies American aspirations and ideals so implacably that she cannot deal with Europe except on the most abstract level. She is so absorbed by an American idealization of the individual, freedom, and moral mission that she loses her sense of reality, just as, for opposite reasons, Osmond has lost his. Europe and America continually stand behind James's conception of the aesthetic Osmond and the moral Isabel; but the implication of the novel for these characters, as well as for the others, is that discrimination and a sense of the relative proportion of things are the final criteria of understanding. An exaggerated perception of one cultural standard or another may lead to a failure of relation to life itself.

James's duality is seen in more than his use of the international theme: it can be seen, indeed, in the sense of life that emerges in the earlier novels. Irving Howe has noted, quite eloquently, that the sense of life in certain of James's novels is at odds with that found in certain other of his novels. He points to *Washington Square, The Portrait of a Lady, What Maisie Knew,* and *The Wings of the Dove* as works "which yield, sometimes with irony but sometimes as pure rhapsody, celebrations of the presence and even the power of goodness." Yet in other works, that include *The Europeans, The Bostonians, The Awkward Age,* and *The Ambassadors,* James writes "as a 'European,' a man very much at home in the world as it is, in all its hardness, polish and cultivation. . . . he acknowledges the power of the given, the durability of institutions, the attractiveness of forms, and the reality of appetites which cannot readily be silenced by moral injunctions. He sees the social world not as a theatre of evil to be destroyed or transcended, but as the arena—the only one we have—in which men act out their lives."

The Europeans is classical in many respects, but in none more than in the impression it gives of the strict finitude of its characters' experience. Europe may offer greater potentialities for self-realization than New England, but what it promises is self-definition through social experience rather than transcendence. Similarly, in

The Bostonians there is no suggestion whatever of its characters being able to transcend their limitations or limited points of view, since they have all been shaped rigidly by their environment. Yet in *Washington Square*, what Howe calls the "power of the given" yields to the sense of the mystery and strength of survival in even the most hostile environment of the inner life; the inner life escapes all effort imposed from without to reduce it to a narrow formulation. In *Watch and Ward*, Roger Lawrence and Nora Lambert move away at the end from the two-dimensional environment in which they have existed toward a more evolved state of being that is not amenable to measurement. Roger is rewarded for his faith and innocence of heart in a world in which these qualities are scorned; and in later, much greater works, innocence becomes a positive force, purifying and redeeming. At the end of *The Portrait of a Lady*, Ralph Touchett's love for Isabel, his unselfish devotion, has a power of spirit that survives his death and blocks any absolutely final judgment of her. In this context, there appear to be not one but two Jameses, one of whom embraces the finitude of experience and is skeptical of the transcendence the other at times urges.

Although not exactly a pragmatist, like his brother William, James is able to entertain different points of view, testing the validity of an assumption from various perspectives. It might be noted in this regard that his characters often "fail" in opposing patterns. Belonging to one pattern are characters who are idealistic and unable to accommodate their idealism with objective experience. A number of such characters appear in James's stories of the 1870s. Theobald in "The Madonna of the Future" (1873) comes to grief because he fails to test his idealistic principles experientially; and Bessie Alden in "An International Episode" (1878) and the heroine in "Madame de Mauves" (1874) can deal with the facts of experience only by attempting to make them conform to their idealistic mode of vision, with the result for Madame de Mauves that her idealism becomes practically life-hating. Isabel Archer's idealism comes to blind her to objective reality, and Olive Chancellor shows the danger of self-deception in an obsessively elevated viewpoint. These characters would give the impression that for James empirical experience rather than abstraction is the ultimate standard by which assumptions must be tested. Yet another line of characters contradict this assumption, for they are defeated through a failure to rise above the objective report of their senses. Neither Roderick Hudson nor Rowland Mallet keeps faith with his ideals, and as a consequence they feel a sense of emptiness and futility at the end. The failure of Christine Light's commitment to spiritual reality earns her only a worldly title and self-contempt, and Madame Merle's betrayal of her higher self brings her nothing at all—except exile and a kind of nonexistence. Characters like Morris Townsend, who can believe only in objective experience are condemned to live in the world and to fail of any transcendence of it.

James's duality could be detailed at length, but what might be noted here is that any simple labeling of him as a novelist would be likely to be inexact. To describe him merely as a "realist," for example, would be misleading since in certain respects he is romantic. Even to call him an "idealistic realist" would need quali-fication, since one of his preoccupations is the self-deception in-volved in idealism. The realism James brings to the earlier novels is problematic. James was preeminently an ironist and analyst of moral problems, and his fiction takes the reader into the mys-teries of the moral life in a way that requires a willingness on the reader's part to participate in the process of understanding and recognition. In James's drama of perception perspectives shift, and there are only tentative apprehensions of order.

Yet values distinctive to James do emerge in the course of the earlier novels. The importance he attaches to "civilization," the civilizing influences that make for complex awareness, is fun-damental to his novels. Equally essential is the unusually large role he assigns to art, which enters into almost all of the earlier novels as background, vocation, or thematic analogue. James's concern with the individual, and his or her inner experience, is central to all of the novels, and his developing conception of the "self" grows out of this concern. In *Watch and Ward*, Roger Lawrence triumphs over his circumstances and his apparently stronger adversaries, Hubert Lawrence and George Fenton, both of whom are selfishly motivated, and have only a worldly conception of self. In *Roderick Hudson*, the principal characters are all defined through their enclosure in self; their inability to get out of themselves, or failure of transcendence, is what they all have in common. In *The American*, on the other hand, Christopher Newman escapes their fate when, turning inward, he discovers a large, new world. Even in these early novels, James's conception of the self, its restriction or expansion, is focal to the fiction; and it continues to be in the other earlier novels.

In *Washington Square*, Catherine Sloper lives without a sense of self until, wounded by her father and lover, she is forced to create one; one that, although small, is able to withstand all pressures from without to distort or corrupt it. The selfish use one character makes of another in *Washington Square* had been witnessed earlier in *Roderick Hudson*, in which Roderick and Christina use one another in order to dramatize their emotions, and in which Rowland uses Roderick, first in living vicariously through him, and then in putting him out of the way in order to have his fiancée.

In *Washington Square*, however, the exploitative use of one character by another becomes a game of the most extraordinary cruelty, in which oppressor characters are blinded to the immorality of their conduct by their egotistic self-involvement. This violation theme is given full orchestration in *The Portrait of a Lady*, in which Osmond becomes a usurper of the inner beings of his wife and child. And in *The Bostonians*, the violation theme appears once again; is exemplified first by Olive, the Back Bay agonist of rectitude, and finally by everyone else in the democratic community. One might say that James's concern with the "self" and the threat of its violation is the dominant theme occurring in the earlier novels. This theme reflects on James's own values. For James, the great "sin," if it can be called that, is pride in self, which narrows or limits consciousness; and the great virtue is transcendence of self, which permits the largest possible outreach to the life of mankind. Such an ethic is curiously similar to Henry James, Sr.'s conception of *proprium*, or the sin of enclosure in self, and redemption through an identity of the self with humanity. James does not necessarily subscribe to his father's theology, but he does seem to have inherited from him a strain of piety, a reverential sense of life in which the drama of selfhood, its narrowing or expansion, has a damning or saving aspect. In this respect, one would have to see James as a moralist, and as the son of a moralist.

The earlier novels have distinction individually; and of these *The Europeans, Washington Square, The Portrait of a Lady,* and *The Bostonians* show James in the fullness of his powers. But their distinction is also collective, for together they create a new literature addressed to the consciously lived life. The inner experience of James's characters is so large and complex, and has an interest so engaging, that it supplants an earlier literature concerned largely with outward events, with plot more than the analysis of character. James's novels do not dispense with plot, but they bring to the novel a new seriousness by focusing upon the human mind. Skeptical as James was of his own characters who were endowed with a sense of mission, he possessed such a sense himself. Almost alone, he redirected the course of later nineteenth-century fiction, redefined it, redefined craft, established a high standard by which achievement in the psychologically oriented novel can be measured. In an industrial and commercial age of cultural impoverishment, James brought "civilization" to America, and redeemed a narrow vision.

Notes and References

The first footnote for each of the main chapters provides a comprehensive survey of criticism dealing with the novel discussed, and is divided, for the reader's convenience, into books, essays discussing revisions, and general essays. Entries in these survey footnotes are bibliographically complete, and subsequent references within the chapter to works cited in the first footnote are given in short form. In this way, the first footnotes for each chapter are self-contained, and constitute a selective bibliography for each of the novels. The separate bibliography that follows these notes and references then supplies a primary bibliography of the printings of the novels, and a selective secondary bibliography of the most important books about James, chosen on the basis of their dealing most fully or directly with the earlier novels.

The specific text of a James novel cited in the discussions is identified in footnotes to the individual chapters. New York Edition texts have been selected where appropriate; in other cases reprints of the first book edition texts are used. In all cases, however, an explanation for the choice of the text is provided.

Chapter One

1. Henry James, Sr., has been treated in F. O. Matthiessen, *The James Family; A Group Portrait* (New York, 1947); Ralph Barton Perry, *The Thought and Character of William James*, vol. 1 (Boston, 1935); C. Hartley Grattan, *The Three Jameses: A Family of Minds* (New York, 1932); and Leon Edel, *Henry James*, 5 vols. (Philadelphia, 1953–72). A selection of his writings in one volume, *The Literary Remains of Henry James* (Boston, 1885), was edited with an introduction by William James; and a modern anthology is Giles

Gunn, ed., *Henry James, Senior: A Selection of his Writings* (Chicago, 1974).

2. The relationship of William and Henry James has been detailed in Matthiessen, *The James Family*; Perry, *The Thought and Character of William James*, vol. 1; and Grattan, *The Three Jameses*. It has been treated more recently, with a Freudian emphasis, in Edel, *Henry James*; and in Gay Wilson Allen, *William James* (New York, 1967).

3. *A Small Boy and Others* (New York, 1913), reprinted in F. W. Dupee, ed., *Henry James: Autobiography* (New York, 1956), pp. 3–236.

4. Quoted in Leon Edel, *Henry James—the Untried Years: 1843–1870* (Philadelphia, 1953), p. 118.

5. *Notes of a Son and Brother* (New York, 1914), reprinted in F. W. Dupee, ed., *Henry James: Autobiography*, pp. 414–15.

6. Quoted in G. W. Allen, *William James*, p. 137.

7. Alice James is treated in Matthiessen, *The James Family*; Perry, *The Thought and Character of William James*; and, more fully, in Edel, *Henry James*. For a recent, full-length biography, see Jean Strouse, *Alice James: A Biography* (Boston, 1980). Leon Edel, ed., *The Diary of Alice James* (New York, 1964) reprints the journal she kept from May, 1889, to March, 1892. See also Ruth Bernard Yeazell, *The Death and Letters of Alice James* (Berkeley, 1980).

8. See G. W. Allen, *William James*, p. 213.

9. The earliest edition of James's letters is Percy Lubbock, ed., *The Letters of Henry James*, 2 vols. (London, 1920), which prints four hundred letters, taken largely from the later period, from several thousand then available. Leon Edel, ed., *Selected Letters of Henry James* (Boston, 1955), is an edition in one volume with a balanced selection from different periods. For the largest and most modern edition of James's letters, see Leon Edel, ed., *Henry James Letters*, vol. 1, *1843–1875*; vol. 2, *1875–1883*; vol. 3, *1883–1895* (Cambridge, Mass., 1974, 1975, 1980). This edition-in-progress draws from over ten thousand letters now available, and is intended to be representative rather than complete.

10. Quoted in F. O. Matthiessen, *The James Family*, p. 126.

11. Ibid., p. 69.

Chapter Two

1. For secondary literature on *Watch and Ward*, see the following. Books: Peter Buitenhuis, *The Grasping Imagination* (Toronto, 1970), pp. 57–66; Oscar Cargill, *The Novels of Henry James* (New York, 1961), pp. 3–18; Leon Edel, *Henry James* (Philadelphia, 1962), 2:42–45; Cornelia Kelley, *The Early Development of Henry James*, rev. ed. (Urbana, Ill., 1965), pp. 122–26; Leo Levy, *Versions of Melodrama* (Berkeley, 1957), pp. 12–18; Donald Mull, *Henry James's "Sublime Economy"* (Middletown, Conn., 1973), pp. 27–30; S. Gorley Putt, *Henry James: A Reader's Guide* (Ithaca, N. Y., 1967), pp. 27–33; Edward Stone, *The Battle and the Books* (Athens, Ohio, 1964, pp. 64–76; William Veeder, *Henry James—the Lessons of the Master* (Chicago, 1975), pp. 73–80, 106–12; J. A. Ward, *The Search for Form* (Chapel Hill, N.C., 1967), pp. 60–76.

Essays discussing revisions: C. Fish, "Form and Revision: The Example of *Watch and Ward*," *Nineteenth-Century Fiction* 22 (1967):178–90; R. McElderry, "Henry James's Revision of *Watch and Ward*," *Modern Language Notes* 67 (1952):457–60.

General Essays: A. Farrer, "Watch, Ward, the Jamesian Themes," *Balcony* 1 (1965):23–27; L. Johnson, "A Dog in the Manger: James's Depiction of Roger Lawrence in *Watch and Ward*," *Arizona Quarterly* 29 (1973):169–76; L. Levy, "The Comedy of *Watch and Ward*," *Arlington Quarterly* 1 (1968):86–98.

2. *Henry James Letters*, 1:110.

3. Ibid., 1:160.

4. Ibid., 1:262.

5. In revising the serial version of *Watch and Ward* for the American book edition of 1878, James made more than eight hundred verbal changes, and many refinements of punctuation; but these changes do not affect fundamental situations or characterizations. The changes tend to make the style simpler and more direct, or to sharpen images and figures.

6. For the critical reception, see Richard Foley, *Criticism in American Periodicals of the Works of Henry James from 1866 to 1916* (Washington, D.C., 1944), pp. 15–16.

7. J. A. Ward, *The Search for Form*, p. 61.

8. In *The Novels of Henry James*, Cargill draws attention to James's possible sources for *Watch and Ward*, citing works by Trol-

lope and George Sand, as well as several by Holmes; but since all of these possibilities are offered as being equally likely, the impression he leaves is one of a vague indefiniteness.

9. The present and all future parenthetical page references are to Henry James, *Watch and Ward* (New York, 1960). This edition, edited by Leon Edel, is the only readily available reprint of the American book edition of 1878. Since James did not revise *Watch and Ward* subsequently or include it in the New York Edition, the American book edition of 1878 remains the definitive text.

10. J. A. Ward, *The Search for Form*, p. 63.

Chapter Three

1. For secondary literature on *Roderick Hudson*, see the following. Books: Charles Anderson, *Person, Place, and Thing in Henry James's Novels* (Durham, N.C., 1977), pp. 9–40; Peter Buitenhuis, *The Grasping Imagination* (Toronto, 1970), pp. 75–84; Oscar Cargill, *The Novels of Henry James* (New York, 1961), pp. 19–40; F. W. Dupee, *Henry James* (New York, 1951), pp. 87–89; Paul John Eakin, *The New England Girl* (Athens, Ga., 1976), pp. 136–42; Leon Edel, *Henry James* (Philadelphia, 1962), 2:175–82; Edward Engelberg, in *Henry James's Major Novels*, ed. Lyall Powers (East Lansing, Mich., 1973), pp. 3–27; Kenneth Graham, *Henry James: The Drama of Fulfillment* (New York, 1975), pp. 29–75; Cornelia Kelley, *The Early Development of Henry James*, rev. ed. (Urbana, Ill., 1965), pp. 182–94; F. R. Leavis, *The Great Tradition* (London, 1948), pp. 160–62; Leo Levy, *Versions of Melodrama* (Berkeley, 1957), pp. 18–21; Ellen Leyburn, *Strange Alloy* (Chapel Hill, N.C., 1968), pp. 11–20; Robert Long, *The Great Succession* (Pittsburgh, 1979), pp. 38–53; Carl Maves, *Sensuous Pessimism* (Bloomington, Ind., 1973), pp. 30–39; Richard Poirier, *The Comic Sense of Henry James* (New York, 1960), pp. 11–43; S. Gorley Putt, *Henry James: A Reader's Guide* (Ithaca, N.Y., 1967), pp. 94–99; Donald Stone, *Novelists in a Changing World* (Cambridge, Mass., 1972), pp. 192–94; William Veeder, *Henry James—the Lessons of the Master* (Chicago, 1975), pp. 90–97; Philip Weinstein, *Henry James & the Requirements of the Imagination* (Cambridge, Mass., 1971), pp. 8–30; Viola Winner, *Henry James and the Visual Arts* (Charlottesville, Va., 1970), pp. 97–108.

Essays discussing revisions: S. Bercovitch, "The Revision of Rowland Mallet," *Nineteenth-Century Fiction* 24 (1969):210–21; H. Harvitt, "How Henry James Revised *Roderick Hudson*," *PMLA* 39 (1924):203–27; R. Havens, "The Revisions of *Roderick Hudson*," *PMLA* 40 (1955):433–34.

General essays: P. Conn, "*Roderick Hudson*: The Role of the Observer," *Nineteenth-Century Fiction* 26 (1971):65–82; V. Dunbar, "A Source for *Roderick Hudson*," *Modern Language Notes* 63 (1948):303–10, and "The Problem in *Roderick Hudson*," *Modern Language Notes* 67 (1952):109–13; R. Gale, "Roderick Hudson and Thomas Crawford," *American Quarterly* 13 (1961):495–504; C. Goodman, "Henry James's *Roderick Hudson* and Nathaniel Parker Willis's *Paul Fane*," *American Literature* 4 (1979):642–45; M. Grenander, "Henry James's *Capricciosa*: Christina Light in *Roderick Hudson* and *The Princess Casamassima*," *PMLA* 75 (1960):309–19; V. Hopkins, "Gloriani and the Tides of Taste," *Nineteenth Century Fiction* 18 (1963):65–71; J. Kraft, " 'Madame de Mauves' and *Roderick Hudson*: The Development of James's International Style," *Texas Quarterly* 2 (1968):143–60; Q. Kraft, "The Central Problem of James's Fictional Thought: from *The Scarlet Letter* to *Roderick Hudson*," *ELH* 36 (1969):416–39; S. Marovitz, "*Roderick Hudson*: James's *Marble Faun*," *Texas Studies in Literature & Language* 11 (1970):427–43; R. Martin, "The 'High Felicity of Comradeship': A New Reading of *Roderick Hudson*," *American Literary Realism* 11 (1978):100–108; E. Nettels, "Action and Point in *Roderick Hudson*," *English Studies* 53 (1978):399–419; L. Snow, " 'The Prose and the Modesty of the Matter': James's Imagery for the Artist in *Roderick Hudson* and *The Tragic Muse*," *Modern Fiction Studies* 12 (1966):61–82; P. Speck, "A Structural Analysis of Henry James's *Roderick Hudson*," *Studies in the Novel* 2 (1970):292–304.

2. *Henry James Letters*, 1:362.

3. When *Roderick Hudson* appeared in book form, it received largely unfavorable reviews. The chief complaints were that the characters were overanalyzed and too minutely portrayed, and that the quality of the writing was wholly without human warmth. Reviews are cited and excerpted in Richard Foley's *Criticism in American Periodicals*, pp. 9–10.

4. For a more detailed discussion of the influence of Turgenev

and Hawthorne on *Roderick Hudson,* see Long, *The Great Succession,* pp. 38–53.

5. Peter Buitenhuis, *The Grasping Imagination,* pp. 75–84.

6. Ibid., p. 81.

7. The present and all future parenthetical page references are to Henry James, *Roderick Hudson* (New York, 1907), the New York Edition, vol. 1. Modern reprints are based either on the first English book edition of 1878 or the New York Edition, but the revised, later version is preferred.

8. Preface to *Roderick Hudson,* in R. P. Blackmur, ed., *The Art of the Novel* (New York, 1934), pp. 13–14.

9. Richard Poirier, *The Comic Sense of Henry James,* p. 12.

10. *The Art of the Novel,* pp. 15–16.

Chapter Four

1. For secondary literature on *The American,* see the following.

Facsimile edition: *Henry James, "The American": The Version of 1877 Revised in Autograph and Transcript for the New York Edition of 1907* (London, 1976).

Critical edition: James W. Tuttleton, ed., *Henry James: "The American": Norton Critical Edition* (New York, 1978).

Critical anthology: William T. Stafford, ed., *Merrill Studies in "The American"* (Columbus, Ohio, 1971).

Books: Charles Anderson, *Person, Place, and Thing in Henry James's Novels* (Durham, N.C., 1977), pp. 41–49; R. W. Butterfield, in *The Air of Reality,* ed. John Goode (London, 1972), pp. 5–35; Oscar Cargill, *The Novels of Henry James* (New York, 1961), pp. 41–61; Leon Edel, *Henry James* (Philadelphia, 1962), 2:110–15; Cornelia Kelley, *The Early Development of Henry James,* rev. ed. (Urbana, Ill., 1965), pp. 234–44; F. R. Leavis, *The Great Tradition* (London, 1948), pp. 173–74; William Maseychik, in *Henry James: Modern Judgements,* ed. Tony Tanner (Middletown, Conn., 1973), pp. 39–44; Elsa Nettels, *James & Conrad* (Athens, Ga., 1977), pp. 84–93; Richard Poirier, *The Comic Sense of Henry James* (New York, 1960), pp. 44–94; Constance Rourke, *American Humor* (New York, 1931), pp. 235–65; Charles Samuels, *The Ambiguity of Henry James* (Urbana, 1971), pp. 41–49; Edward Stone, *The Battle and the Books*

(Lincoln, Neb., 1961), pp. 39–43; Viola Winner, *Henry James and the Visual Arts* (Charlottesville, Va., 1970), pp. 129–33.

Essays discussing revisions: R. Gettmann, "Henry James's Revisions of *The American*," *American Literature* 16 (1945):279–95; R. Pearce, Introduction, to the *The American* (Boston, 1962), pp. i–xxv; L. Reynolds, "Henry James's New Christopher Newman," *Texas Studies in Literature & Language* 16 (1974):329–47; M. Schulz, "The Bellegardes' Feud with Christopher Newman: A Study of Henry James's Revision of *The American*," *American Literature* 27 (1955):42–55; W. Stafford, "The Ending of James's *The American*: A Defense of the Early Version," *Nineteenth-Century Fiction* 18 (1963):86–89; I. Traschen, "Henry James and the Art of Revision," *Philological Quarterly* 35 (1956):39–47, and "James's Revisions of the Love Affair in *The American*," *New England Quarterly* 29 (1956):43–62; F. Watkins, "Christopher Newman's Final Instinct," *Nineteenth Century Fiction* 12 (1957):85–88.

General essays: J. Antush, "The 'Much Finer Complexity' of History in *The American*," *Journal of American Studies* 6 (1972):85–95; M. Blasing, "Double Focus in *The American*," *Nineteenth-Century Fiction* 28 (1973):74–84; C. Brooks, "The American 'Innocence,'" *Shenandoah* 16 (1964):21–37; N. De Loasch, "The Influence of William James on the Composition of *The American*," *Interpretations* 7 (1975):38–43; G. Knox, "Romance and Fable in James's *The American*," *Anglia* 83 (1965):308–23; M. Kotzin, "*The American* and *The Newcomes*," *Etudes Anglaises* 30 (1977):420–29; H. Lang, "The Making of *The American*: The contributions of Four Literatures," *Jahrbuch für Amerikastudien* 20 (1975):58–71; R. McMaster, "'An Honorable Emulation of the Author of *The Newcomes*': James and Thackeray," *Nineteenth-Century Fiction* 32 (1978):399–419; L. Person, "Aesthetic Headaches and European Woman in *The Marble Faun* and *The American*," *Studies in American Fiction* 4 (1976): 65–79; R. Secor, "Christopher Newman: How Innocent is James's American?," *Studies in Short Fiction* 1 (1973):143–53; S. Tick, "Henry James's *The American: Voyons*," *Studies in the Novel* 2 (1970):276–91; S. Ward, "Painting and Europe in *The American*," *American Literature* 46 (1975):566–73; J. Wilson, "The Gospel According to Christopher Newman," *Studies in American Fiction* 3 (1975):83–88.

2. The columns have since been collected in Leon Edel and Ilse Dusoir Lind, eds., *Parisian Sketches: Letters to the New York "Tribune" 1875–76* (London, 1958).

3. *Henry James Letters*, 2:484.

4. Certain incidents and settings in the novel also had some basis in fact. James's brief impressions at a ducal reception contributed to the scene in which the Bellegardes receive the Parisian *noblesse* at their home. And the country home of the Bellegardes at Fleurières, was adapted from James's observations of a moated chateau at Amilly, which he visited in August, 1876, while still at work on the novel.

5. The critical reception of *The American* is detailed in Richard Foley's *Criticism in American Periodicals*, pp. 10–13. For the reception of the novel in England, see Roger Gard, ed., *Henry James: The Critical Heritage* (London, 1968), p. 45. Specimen reviews, both English and American, are reprinted in *The Merrill Studies in "The American,"* pp. 25–32; and *Henry James: "The American": Norton Critical Edition*, pp. 390–410. In general reviewers were enthusiastic, and considered *The American* a distinct advance over *Roderick Hudson*. The criticism continued to be made, however, of a lack of emotional warmth in James's writing, of an excessively detached, analytical attitude toward his characters.

6. The writing, staging, and reception of the play are discussed by Leon Edel in *The Complete Plays of Henry James* (Philadelphia, 1949), pp. 179–90. The text of the play, *"The American": In Four Acts*, is also printed in the volume, pp. 192–242.

7. *The Art of the Novel*, pp. 21–22.

8. The present and all future parenthetical page references are to J. W. Tuttleton, ed., *Henry James: "The American": Norton Critical Edition* (New York, 1978), which reprints the text of the first English book edition of 1879. James later revised *The American* for the New York Edition, but for greater sharpness and spontaneity, the earlier text is preferred by most critics. The text cited is selected over other reprints for its accuracy and its special appendix showing revisions made by James from the serial and first American book texts.

9. Quoted in F. O. Matthiessen, *The James Family*, p. 343.

10. *Notebooks*, p. 26.

11. *The Art of the Novel*, p. 34.

Chapter Five

1. For secondary literature on *The Europeans*, see the following.
Facsimile edition: *Henry James, "The Europeans": A Facsimile of the Manuscript* (New York, 1978).

Books: Peter Buitenhuis, *The Grasping Imagination* (Toronto, 1970), pp. 89–102; Oscar Cargill, *The Novels of Henry James* (New York, 1961), pp. 62–72; F. W. Dupee, *Henry James* (New York, 1951), pp. 100–104; Paul Eakin, *The New England Girl* (Athens, Ga., 1976), pp. 142–57; Leon Edel, *Henry James* (Philadelphia, 1962), 2:313–15; Charles Hoffmann, *The Short Novels of Henry James* (New York, 1957), pp. 37–40; Cornelia Kelley, *The Early Development of Henry James*, rev. ed. (Urbana, Ill., 1965), pp. 261–64; F. R. Leavis, *The Great Tradition* (London, 1948), pp. 170–73; Leo Levy, *Versions of Melodrama* (Berkeley, 1957), pp. 33–35; Robert Long, *The Great Succession* (Pittsburgh, 1979), pp. 54–63; Donald Mull, *Henry James's "Sublime Economy"* (Middletown, Conn., 1973), pp. 44–47; Richard Poirier, *The Comic Sense of Henry James* (New York, 1960), pp. 95–144; Lyall Powers, *Henry James: An Introduction* (New York, 1970), pp. 54–57; S. Gorley Putt, *Henry James: A Reader's Guide* (Ithaca, N.Y., 1967), pp. 115–19; Charles Samuels, *The Ambiguity of Henry James* (Urbana, 1971), pp. 131–38; Sallie Sears, *The Negative Imagination* (Ithaca, N.Y., 1963), pp. 3–16; Donald Stone, *Novelists in a Changing World* (Cambridge, Mass., 1972), pp. 198–99; J. A. Ward, *The Search for Form* (Chapel Hill, 1967), pp. 95–113; Viola Winner, *Henry James and the Visual Arts* (Charlottesville, Va., 1970), pp. 103–35.

Essays: D. Austin, "Innocents at Home: A Study of *The Europeans* of Henry James," *Journal of General Education* 14 (1962):103–29; F. Leavis, "The Novel as Dramatic Poem: *The Europeans,*" *Scrutiny* 15 (1948):209–21; J. Tuttleton, "Propriety and Fine Perception: James's *The Europeans,*" *Modern Language Review* 73 (1978):481–95; H. Vandemoere, "Baroness Münster's Failure," *English Studies* 50 (1969):47–57.

2. *Henry James Letters*, 2:106.
3. Ibid., 2:189.
4. See Richard Foley, *Criticism in American Periodicals*, pp. 16–20.
5. *Henry James Letters*, 2:193.

6. Thomas Wentworth Higginson, "Henry James, Jr.," *Literary World* 10 (November 22, 1879):383–84; reprinted in *The Question of Henry James*, ed. F. W. Dupee (New York, 1945), pp. 3–4.

7. F. R. Leavis, *The Great Tradition*, p. 173.

8. *Henry James Letters*, 2:189.

9. The present and all future parenthetical page references are to *The Europeans*, in *The American Novels and Stories of Henry James*, ed. F. O. Matthiessen (New York, 1947), pp. 37–161. This text, which reprints the first American book edition of 1878, is selected for accuracy and availability. *The Europeans* was not revised subsequently for the New York Edition.

10. Quoted in Leon Edel, *Henry James*, 2:315.

Chapter Six

1. For secondary literature on *Confidence*, see the following.

Critical edition: Herbert Ruhm, ed., *Henry James: "Confidence"* (New York, 1962).

Books: Oscar Cargill, *The Novels of Henry James* (New York, 1961), pp. 73–77; Charles Hoffmann, *The Short Novels of Henry James* (New York, 1957), pp. 37–43; Cornelia Kelley, *The Early Development of Henry James*, rev. ed. (Urbana, Ill., 1965), pp. 275–78; Leo Levy, *Versions of Melodrama* (Berkeley, 1957), pp. 36–40; Bruce McElderry, *Henry James* (New York, 1960), pp. 145–64; S. Gorley Putt, *Henry James: A Reader's Guide* (Ithaca, N.Y., 1965), pp. 100–104; Donald Stone, *Novelists in a Changing World* (Cambridge, Mass., 1972), pp. 199–200.

Essays: M. Collins, "The Center of Consciousness on Stage: Henry James's *Confidence*," *Studies in American Fiction* 3 (1975):39–50; A. Hamblen, "*Confidence*: The Surprising Shadow of Genius," *University Review* 36 (1969):151–54; L. Levy, "Henry James's *Confidence* and the Development of the Idea of the Unconscious," *American Literature* 28 (1956):347–58.

2. *Henry James Letters*, 2:231.

3. For the critical reception, see Richard Foley, *Criticism in American Periodicals*, p. 23. Nine of the original reviews are extracted in Herbert Ruhm, ed., *Henry James, "Confidence,"* pp. 218–29.

4. Herbert Ruhm, ed., *Henry James, "Confidence,"* p. 228.

5. Oscar Cargill, *The Novels of Henry James*, p. 74.

6. *Notebooks*, pp. 3–6.

7. The present and all future parenthetical page references are to Herbert Ruhm, ed., *Henry James: "Confidence."* The text cited is the only edition of *Confidence* readily available today, and reprints the first American book edition of 1880, together with a notation of all changes made in the course of revision from the manuscript and serialized version. *Confidence* was not included in the New York Edition.

8. For secondary literature on *Washington Square*, see the following.

Books: Edwin Bowden, *The Themes of Henry James* (New Haven, 1956), pp. 41–42; Peter Buitenhuis, *The Grasping Imagination* (Toronto, 1970), pp. 106–8; F. W. Dupee, *Henry James* (New York, 1951), pp. 63–65; Leon Edel, *Henry James*, vol. 2 (Philadelphia, 1962), pp. 397–402; Charles Hoffmann, *The Short Novels of Henry James* (New York, 1957), pp. 25–37; Cornelia Kelley, *The Early Development of Henry James*, rev. ed. (Urbana, Ill., 1965), pp. 278–83; Leo Levy, *Versions of Melodrama* (Berkeley, 1957), pp. 38–40; Robert Long, *The Great Succession* (Pittsburgh, 1979), pp. 83–97; J. Lucas, in *The Air of Reality*, ed. John Goode (London, 1972), pp. 36–59; Elsa Nettels, *James & Conrad* (Athens, Ga., 1977), pp. 95–97; Richard Poirier, *The Comic Sense of Henry James* (New York, 1960), pp. 165–82; S. Gorley Putt, *Henry James: A Reader's Guide* (Ithaca, N.Y., 1966), pp. 46–51; Charles Samuels, *The Ambiguity of Henry James* (Urbana, 1971), pp. 141–49; Mary Springer, *A Rhetoric of Literary Character* (Chicago, 1978), pp. 77–89; Donald Stone, *Novelists in a Changing World* (Cambridge, Mass., 1972), pp. 201–4; William Veeder, *Henry James—the Lessons of the Master* (Chicago, 1975), pp. 184–206.

Essays: M. Bell, "Style as Subject: *Washington Square*," *Sewanee Review* 83 (1975):19–38; G. Cambon, "The Negative Gesture in Henry James," *Nineteenth-Century Fiction* 15 (1961):335–43; J. Gargano, "*Washington Square*: A Study in the Growth of an Inner Self," *Studies in Short Fiction* 13 (1976):336–62; R. Johannsen, "Two Sides of *Washington Square*," *South Carolina Review* 6 (1974): 60–65; W. Kenney, "Doctor Sloper's Double in *Washington Square*," *University Review* 36 (1970):301–6; D. Maini, "*Washington Square*: A Centennial Essay," *Henry James Review* 1 (1979):81–101; H.

Schecter, "The Unpardonable Sin in *Washington Square*," *Studies in Short Fiction* 10 (1973):137–41.

    9. *Henry James Letters*, 2:268.

    10. Ibid., 2:308.

    11. Ibid., 2:316.

    12. Leon Edel, ed., *The Selected Letters of Henry James* (New York, 1955), p. 159.

    13. See Richard Foley, *Criticism in American Periodicals*, pp. 24–25.

    14. Ibid., p. 24.

    15. Ibid.

    16. Ibid.

    17. C. Hartley Grattan, *The Three Jameses*, p. 263.

    18. J. I. M. Stewart, *Eight Modern Writers*, p. 93.

    19. Rebecca West, *Henry James* (New York, 1916), p. 55.

    20. Morton Zabel, *Craft and Character in Modern Fiction* (New York, 1957), p. 131.

    21. Donald Stone, *Novelists in a Changing World*, p. 204.

    22. *Notebooks*, pp. 12–13.

    23. *The American Scene* (1907; reprint ed., New York, 1967), p. 57.

    24. The present and all future parenthetical page references are to Henry James, *Washington Square*, in *The American Novels and Stories of Henry James*, ed. F. O. Matthiessen (New York, 1947), pp. 162–295. The text cited reprints the first English book edition of 1881, and is selected for accuracy and ready availability. *Washington Square* was not subsequently revised or included in the New York Edition.

    25. For a more detailed discussion of the relation of "Rappaccini's Daughter" to *Washington Square*, see Long, *The Great Succession*, pp. 83–97.

    26. Robert L. Gale, *The Caught Image* (Chapel Hill, N.C., 1964), p. 98.

Chapter Seven

    1. For secondary literature on *The Portrait of a Lady*, see the following.

Critical edition: Robert D. Bamberg, ed., *"The Portrait of a Lady"*:

An Authoritative Text; Henry James and the Novel; Reviews and Criticism (New York, 1975).

Books entirely on "The Portrait": Peter Buitenhuis, ed., *Twentieth Century Interpretations of "The Portrait of a Lady"* (Englewood Cliffs, N.J., 1968); David Galloway, *Henry James: "The Portrait of a Lady"* (London, 1967); Lyall Powers, ed., *The Merrill Studies in "The Portrait of a Lady"* (Columbus, Ohio, 1970); William T. Stafford, ed., *Perspectives on "The Portrait of a Lady": A Collection of Critical Essays* (New York, 1967).

Sections of books: Charles Anderson, *Person, Place and Thing in Henry James's Novels* (Durham, N.C., 1977), pp. 80–123; Martha Banta, *Henry James and the Occult* (Bloomington, Ind., 1972), pp. 169–78; Peter Buitenhuis, *The Grasping Imagination* (Toronto, 1970), pp. 103–12; Oscar Cargill, *The Novels of Henry James* (New York, 1961), pp. 78–119; Richard Chase, *The American Novel and its Tradition* (New York, 1957), pp. 117–37; F. W. Dupee, *Henry James* (New York, 1951), pp. 113–25; Paul Eakin, *The New England Girl* (Athens, Ga., 1976), pp. 168–94; Leon Edel, *Henry James*, vol. 2 (Philadelphia, 1962), pp. 417–32; L. B. Holland, *The Expense of Vision* (Princeton, 1964), pp. 3–54; Cornelia Kelley, *The Early Development of Henry James,* rev. ed. (Urbana, Ill., 1965), pp. 284–300; Arnold Kettle, *An Introduction to the English Novel,* vol. 2 (London, 1953), pp. 13–34; Dorothea Krook, *The Ordeal of Consciousness in Henry James* (London, 1962), pp. 26–61, 357–69; F. R. Leavis, *The Great Tradition* (London, 1948), pp. 179–87; Naomi Lebowitz, *The Imagination of Loving* (Detroit, 1965), pp. 64–86; Leo Levy, *Versions of Melodrama* (Berkeley, 1957), pp. 40–52; Robert Long, *The Great Succession* (Pittsburgh, 1979), pp. 98–117; Carl Maves, *Sensuous Pessimism* (Bloomington, Ind., 1973), pp. 72–80; Donald Mull, *Henry James's "Sublime Economy"* (Middletown, Conn., 1973), pp. 48–115; Elsa Nettels, *James & Conrad* (Athens, Ga., 1977), pp. 100–107; Richard Poirier, *The Comic Sense of Henry James* (New York, 1960), pp. 183–246, Lyall Powers, *Henry James: An Introduction* (New York, 1970), pp. 60–75; S. Gorley Putt, *Henry James: A Reader's Guide* (Ithaca, N.Y., 1967), pp. 137–60; Philip Rahv, *Image and Idea* (New York, 1959), pp. 62–69; Charles Samuels, *The Ambiguity of Henry James* (Urbana, Ill., 1971), pp. 108–28; Ora Segal, *The Lucid Reflector* (New Haven, 1969), pp. 33–55; Sister M. Sharp, *The Confidante in Henry James* (South Bend,

Ind., 1963), pp. 67–96; Robert Stallman, *The Houses That James Built* (East Lansing, Mich., 1961), pp. 1–33; J. I. M. Stewart, *Eight Modern Writers* (Cambridge, Mass., 1972), pp. 206–28; H. Peter Stowell, *Literary Impressionism, James and Chekhov* (Athens, Ga., 1980), pp. 177–85; Tony Tanner, in *Modern Judgements*, ed. Tanner (London, 1968), pp. 143–59; Dorothy Van Ghent, *The English Novel* (New York, 1953), pp. 211–28, 428–39; William Veeder, *Henry James—The Lessons of the Master* (Cambridge, Mass., 1971), pp. 31–71; Viola Winner, *Henry James and the Visual Arts* (Charlottesville, Va., 1970), pp. 135–43.

Essays discussing revisions: D. Krause, "James's Revisions of the Style of *The Portrait of a Lady*," *American Literature* 30 (1968):57–88; F. Matthiessen, "The Painter's Sponge and Varnish Bottle," in his *Henry James: The Major Phase*, pp. 152–86; A. Mazzella, "The New Isabel," in Bamberg, ed., *"The Portrait of a Lady": An Authoritative Text*, pp. 597–617.

General essays: D. Bazzanella, "The Conclusion to *The Portrait of a Lady* Re-examined," *American Literature* 41 (1969):55–63; H. Blodgett, "Verbal Clues in *The Portrait of a Lady*: A Note in Defense of Isabel Archer," *Studies in American Fiction* 7 (1979):27–36; J. Bochner, "Life in a Picture Gallery: 'Things' in *The Portrait of a Lady* and *The Marble Faun*," *Texas Studies in Literature & Language* 11 (1969):761–77; C. Feidelson, "The Moment of *The Portrait of a Lady*," *Nineteenth-Century Fiction* 20 (1965):85–95; M. Grenander et al., "The Time-Scheme in *The Portrait of a Lady*," *American Literature* 32 (1960):127–35; G. Levine, "Isabel, Gwendolen, & Dorothea," *ELH* 30 (1963):244–57; S. Liebman, "The Light and the Dark: Character Design in *The Portrait of a Lady*," *Papers on Language & Literature* 6 (1970):163–79; M. Mackenzie, "Ironic Melodrama in *The Portrait of a Lady*," *Modern Fiction Studies* 12 (1966):7–23; J. McMaster, "The Portrait of Isabel Archer," *American Literature* 45 (1973):50–66; M. Montgomery, "The Flaw in the Portrait: Henry James vs. Isabel Archer," *University of Kansas City Review* 26 (1960):215–20; A. Niowtzow, "Marriage & the New Woman in *The Portrait of a Lady*," *American Literature* 47 (1975): 377–95; M. Perloff, "Cinderella Becomes the Wicked Step-Mother: *The Portrait of a Lady* as an Ironic Fairy Tale," *Nineteenth-Century Fiction* 23 (1968):413–33; S. Reid, "Moral Passion in *The Portrait of a Lady* and *The Spoils of Poynton*," *Modern Fiction Studies* 12

Notes and References 177

(1966):24–43; J. Rodenbeck, "The Bolted Door in James's *The Portrait of a Lady*," *Modern Fiction Studies* 10 (1965):330–40; E. Sandeen, "*The Wings of the Dove* and *The Portrait of a Lady*: A Study of Henry James's Later Phase," *PMLA* 69 (1954):1064–78; L. Snow, "The Disconcerting Poetry of Mary Temple: a Comparison of the Imagery of *The Portrait of a Lady* and *The Wings of a Dove*," *New England Quarterly* 21 (1958):312–39; S. Stambough, "The Aesthetic Movement and *The Portrait of a Lady*," *Nineteenth-Century Fiction* 30 (1976):495–510; W. Stein, "*The Portrait of a Lady*: *Vis Inertiae*," *Western Humanities Review* 13 (1959):177–90; J. Treadwell, "Mrs. Touchett's Three Questions," *American Literature* 50 (1979):641–44.

2. *Notebooks*, p. 29.

3. *Henry James Letters*, 2:29.

4. American reviews are listed and characterized in Richard Foley, *Criticism in American Periodicals*, pp. 25–29; English critical reception is discussed in Roger Gard, ed., *Henry James: The Critical Heritage*, pp. 5–10. Some of the contemporary reviews are extracted in W. T. Stafford, ed., *Perspectives on James's "The Portrait of a Lady*," pp. 30–34; L. Powers, ed., *Merrill Studies in "The Portrait of a Lady*," pp. 1–18; and R. D. Bamberg, ed., *"The Portrait of a Lady": An Authoritative Text*, pp. 655–63.

5. W. C. Brownell, "James's *The Portrait of a Lady*," *Nation* (February 2, 1882); reprinted in R. Bamberg, ed., *"The Portrait of a Lady": An Authoritative Text*, p. 651.

6. John Hay, "James's *The Portrait of a Lady*," *New York Tribune*, December 25, 1881; reprinted in L. Powers, ed., *Merrill Studies*, pp. 1–7.

7. The present and all future parenthetical page references are to *The Portrait of a Lady* (New York, 1907–9), the New York Edition, vols. 3–4. This edition is considered definitive, and is used in virtually all reprints of the novel.

8. For a good, concise study of Turgenev and James, see Daniel Lerner, "The Influence of Turgenev on Henry James," *Slavonic and East European Review* 20 (December, 1941):23–54.

9. Henry James, "Ivan Turgenieff," in *French Poets and Novelists* (1878; reprint ed., New York, 1964), p. 225.

10. For more detailed discussions of George Eliot and *The Portrait of a Lady*, see F. R. Leavis, *The Great Tradition*, pp. 101–54; Robert

Long, *The Great Succession*, pp. 98–104; and G. Levine, "Isabel, Gwendolyn, and Dorothea," *ELH* 30 (1963):244–57.

11. For a discussion of *The Portrait of a Lady* in relation to literary Impressionism, see H. Peter Stowell, *Literary Impressionism, James and Chekhov*, pp. 177–85.

12. Lyall Powers, "*The Portrait of a Lady*: 'The Eternal Mystery of Things,'" *Nineteenth-Century Fiction* 14 (1959):143–55; reprinted in Powers, ed., *Henry James's Major Novels: Essays in Criticism*, pp. 73–85. See also Powers, *Henry James: An Introduction and Interpretation*, pp. 60–75.

Chapter Eight

1. For secondary literature on *The Bostonians*, see the following.

Critical edition: Alfred Habegger, ed., *Henry James: "The Bostonians"* (Indianapolis, Ind., 1976).

Books: Martha Banta, *Henry James and the Occult* (Bloomington, Ind., 1972), pp. 169–78; Marius Bewley, *The Complex Fate* (London, 1952), pp. 11–31; Peter Buitenhuis, *The Grasping Imagination*, pp. 141–59; Oscar Cargill, *The Novels of Henry James* (New York, 1951), pp. 149–53; Paul Eakin, *The New England Girl* (Athens, Ga., 1976), pp. 195–217; Leon Edel, *Henry James*, vol. 3 (Philadelphia, 1962), pp. 137–46; David Howard, in *The Air of Reality*, ed. John Goode (London, 1972), pp. 60–80; Irving Howe, introduction to the *The Bostonians* (New York, 1956), pp. i–xxviii; Howard Kerr, *Mediums, and Spirit-Rappers, and Roaring Radicals* (Urbana, 1972), pp. 180–219; F. R. Leavis, *The Great Tradition* (London, 1948), pp. 162–70; Leo Levy, *Versions of Melodrama* (Berkeley, 1957), pp. 58–62; R. W. B. Lewis, *Trials of the Word* (New Haven, 1965), pp. 77–96; Robert Long, *The Great Succession* (Pittsburgh, 1979), pp. 117–58; William McMurray, in Tony Tanner, ed., *Henry James: Modern Judgements* (London, 1968), pp. 160–65; Sergio Perosa, *Henry James and the Experimental Novel* (East Lansing, Mich., 1971), pp. 42–87; S. Gorley Putt, *Henry James: A Reader's Guide* (Ithaca, N.Y., 1967), pp. 178–94; Charles Samuels, *The Ambiguity of Henry James* (Urbana, Ill., 1971), pp. 91–107; Donald Stone, *Novelists in a Changing World* (Cambridge, Mass., 1972), pp. 255–82; Lionel Trilling, *The Opposing Self* (New York, 1955), pp. 104–17; Charles Walcutt, *Man's Changing Mask* (Minneapolis, 1966), pp. 182–86.

Essays: C. Anderson, "James's Portrait of the Southerner," *American Literature* 27 (1955):309–31; G. Burns, *"The Bostonians,"* *Critical Quarterly* 13 (1969): 45–60; S. Davis, "Feminist Sources in *The Bostonians,"* *American Literature* 50 (1979):570–87; D. Green, "Witch and Bewitchment in *The Bostonians,"* *Papers on Language & Literature* 3 (1967):267–69; A. Habbeger, "The Disunity of *The Bostonians,"* *Nineteenth-Century Fiction* 24 (1969): 193–209; A. Hamblen, "Henry James and the Freedom Fighters of the Seventies," *Georgia Review* 20 (1966):35–44; M. Hartsock, "Henry James and the Cities of the Plain," *Modern Language Quarterly* 29 (1968):297–311; D. Heaton, "The Altered Consciousness of Miss Birdseye in Henry James's *The Bostonians,"* *American Literature* 50 (1979):588–603; M. Jacobsen, "Popular Fiction and Henry James's Unpopular *Bostonians,"* *Modern Philology* 73 (1976):264–75; L. Johnson, "The Psychology of Characterization: James's Portrait of Verena Tarrant and Olive Chancellor," *Studies in the Novel* 6 (1974):295–303; J. Kimmey, *"The Bostonians* and *The Princess Casamassima,"* *Texas Studies in Literature & Language* 9 (1968):537–46; W. Martin, "The Use of Fairy-Tale: A Note on the Structure of *The Bostonians,"* *English Studies in Africa* 2 (1959):98–109; R. McLean, *"The Bostonians:* New England Pastoral," *Papers on Literature & Language* 7 (1971): 374–81; C. McMahan, "Sexual Desire and Illusion in *The Bostonians,"* *Modern Fiction Studies* 25 (1979): 241–51; T. Miller, "The Muddled Politics of Henry James's *The Bostonians,"* *Georgia Review* 26 (1972):336–46; R. Morris, "Classical Vision and the American City: Henry James's *The Bostonians,"* *New England Quarterly* 46 (1973): 543–57; P. Page, "The Curious Narration of *The Bostonians,"* *American Literature* 46 (1974):37–83; H. D. Pearce, "Witchcraft Imagery and Allusion in James's *Bostonians,"* *Studies in the Novel* 6 (1974): 236–47; L. Powers, "James's Debt to Alphone Daudet," *Comparative Literature* 24 (1972):150–62; E. Schultz, *"The Bostonians:* The Contagion of Romantic Illusion," *Genre* 4 (1971):45–59; R. Selig, "The Red Haired Orator: Parallel Passages in *The Bostonians* and *Adam Bede,"* *Nineteenth-Century Fiction* 16 (1962):539–44; S. Wolstenholme, "Possession and Personality: Spiritualism in *The Bostonians,"* *American Literature* 49 (1979):580–91.

2. Quoted in Edel, *Henry James*, 3:44.

3. See Richard Foley, *Criticism in American Periodicals*, pp. 39–40.

4. Quoted in Oscar Cargill, *The Novels of Henry James*, p. 133.

5. *Letters* 2:100.

6. Ibid., 2:498.

7. Mildred Howells, ed., *Life in Letters of William Dean Howells*, 2:279.

8. Carl Van Doren, *The American Novel: 1789–1939* (New York, 1940), p. 175.

9. Joseph Warren Beach, *The Method of Henry James*, rev. ed. (Philadelphia, 1954), p. 226.

10. F. R. Leavis, *The Great Tradition*, p. 169.

11. *Henry James Letters*, 1:103.

12. Leon Edel, ed., *Henry James: The American Essays*, p. 156.

13. *Notebooks*, p. 47.

14. For discussions of Daudet and *The Bostonians*, see Lyall Powers, *Henry James and the Naturalist Movement*, pp. 42–87, and "James's Debt to Daudet," *Comparative Literature* 24 (1972):150–62; Peter Buitenhuis, *The Grasping Imagination*, pp. 141–59; and Robert Long, *The Great Succession*, pp. 121–22, 148, 190.

15. On Howells and *The Bostonians*, see Long, *The Great Succession*, pp. 139–57.

16. For discussions of *The Blithedale Romance* and *The Bostonians*, see Marius Bewley, *The Complex Fate*, pp. 11–31; and Robert Long, *The Great Succession*, pp. 117–57.

17. The present and all future parenthetical page references are to *The Bostonians* (New York, 1945), which reprints the English book edition of 1886. *The Bostonians* was not included in the New York Edition, or subsequently revised. The text cited is selected for accuracy and ready availability.

18. *The American Scene*, p. 10.

19. Leon Edel, ed., *Henry James: The American Essays*, p. 64.

20. Quoted in George Monteiro, *Henry James and John Hay: the Record of a Friendship* (Providence, R.I., 1965), p. 97.

21. Graham Burns, "*The Bostonians*," *Critical Quarterly* 13 (1969):54.

22. Lyall Powers, *Henry James & the Naturalist Movement*, p. 87.

Selected Bibliography

PRIMARY SOURCES

This bibliography is selective, covering only the novels published to *The Bostonians*. Other writings of James related to the novels are cited in footnotes, with full bibliographical information. Of primary relevance among these materials are the short stories, forty-seven of which were published in the earlier period, all of them included in the first six volumes of the twelve-volume *The Complete Tales of Henry James*, edited by Leon Edel. Relevant, also, are James's notebooks and letters; a modern edition of the letters, edited by Leon Edel is in progress, with the first three volumes now published, covering the years 1843–1895. James's literary criticism of the earlier period was published principally in his *French Poets and Novelists, Hawthorne, The Art of Fiction,* and *Partial Portraits*; his reviews of books have been published posthumously in a number of separate collections. His chief travel books of the earlier period were *Transatlantic Sketches* and *Portraits of Places*; and his early writing on the fine arts and Parisian society have been collected posthumously as *The Painter's Eye* and *Parisian Sketches*, respectively. Complete information pertaining to James's publication may be found in *A Bibliography of Henry James*, rev. ed. (London, 1961), edited by Leon Edel and Dan Laurence.

Watch and Ward. Atlantic Monthly, August–December, 1871. First book publication (revised), Boston: Houghton, Osgood & Co., 1878.

Roderick Hudson. Atlantic Monthly, January–December, 1875. First

American book pub., Boston: James R. Osgood & Co., 1876; first
English edition (revised), London: Macmillan & Co., 1879. Revised for the New York Edition (1907–9), vol. 1.

The American. Atlantic Monthly, June, 1876–May, 1877. First American edition, Boston: James R. Osgood & Co., 1877; first au-
thorized English edition, London: Macmillan & Co., 1879. Revised for the New York Edition (1907–9), vol. 2.

The Europeans: A Sketch. Atlantic Monthly, July–October, 1878. First
American edition, Boston: Houghton & Co., 1878; first English
edition, London: Macmillan & Co., 1878.

Confidence. Scribner's Monthly, August, 1879–January, 1880. First
American edition, Boston: Houghton, Osgood & Co., 1880; first
English edition, Chatto & Windus, 1879.

Washington Square. Cornhill Magazine, June–November, 1880, and
in *Harper's New Monthly Magazine*, July–December, 1880. First
American edition, New York: Harper & Bros., 1880; first English
edition, London: Macmillan & Co., 1881.

The Portrait of a Lady. Macmillan's Magazine, October, 1880–November, 1881, and in *Atlantic Monthly*, November, 1880–December,
1881. First American edition, Boston: Houghton, Mifflin & Co.,
1881; first English edition, London: Macmillan & Co., 1881. Revised for the New York Edition (1907–9), vols. 3 & 4.

The Bostonians. Century Magazine, February, 1885–February, 1886.
First American edition, New York: Macmillan & Co., 1886; first
English edition, London: Macmillan & Co., 1886.

SECONDARY SOURCES

This section identifies books most closely related to the earlier
novels, with emphasis on critical rather than biographical studies. No
works devoted wholly to the later period are included. For more
comprehensive surveys of the secondary literature on James, see
Beatrice Ricks, ed., *Henry James: A Bibliography of Secondary Works*
(Metuchen, N.J., 1975); Kristan Pruitt McColgan, ed., *Henry James,
1917–1959: A Reference Guide* (Boston, 1979); and Dorothy Mc-
Innis Scura, ed., *Henry James 1960–1974: A Reference Guide* (Boston, 1980). For a comprehensive yet concise survey, see Robert L.

Gale, "Henry James," in *Eight American Authors*, ed. James Woodress (New York, 1971), pp. 321–75.

Anderson, Charles R. *Person, Place, and Thing in Henry James's Novels*. Durham, N.C.: Duke University Press, 1977. Traces James's use of "things"—houses, works of art, etc.—from peripheral to central role in the psychology of perception in James's novels. Lengthy chapters on *Roderick Hudson, The American*, and *The Portrait of a Lady*.

Bamberg, Robert D., ed. *"The Portrait of a Lady": An Authoritative Text; Henry James and the Novel; Reviews and Criticism*. New York: W. W. Norton & Co., 1975. Contains the text of the New York Edition, with an appendix noting all changes made in revision from the book edition of 1881; selection of contemporary reviews and recent criticism; and an extensive bibliography of secondary literature on *The Portrait*.

Banta, Martha. *Henry James and the Occult: the Great Extension*. Bloomington: Indiana University Press, 1972. Spiritualism in relation to William and Henry James, with focus on James's ghostly tales. Contains sections on *The Portrait of a Lady* and *The Bostonians*.

Bewley, Marius. *The Complex Fate: Hawthorne, Henry James, And Some Other American Writers*. London: Chatto & Windus, 1952. Idiosyncratic, suggestive essays concerned with James and his major American predecessors in the novel in relation to the culture of Europe; contains several pioneering chapters on the James-Hawthorne relationship.

Buitenhuis, Peter. *The Grasping Imagination: The American Writings of Henry James*. Toronto: University of Toronto Press, 1970. Sensitive treatment of James's fiction having an American setting, with chapters on *Watch and Ward, Roderick Hudson, The Europeans*, and *The Bostonians*.

Cargill, Oscar. *The Novels of Henry James*. New York: Macmillan, 1961. Survey of James's novels with emphasis on source and influence and critical controversies. Still useful, although the background material is out of date, and the criticism is sketchy. All the earlier novels, except *Washington Square*, are covered.

Dupee, F. W. *Henry James*. New York: William Sloane, 1951. The best account of James's life and career in a single volume; but the novels are treated only glancingly.

Eakin, Paul John. *The New England Girl: Cultural Ideals in Hawthorne, Stowe, Howells and James.* Athens: University of Georgia Press, 1976. Observant study of the New England girl as reflector of cultural ideals, from early conceptions of her capacity to ennoble life to the scaling down of her redemptive possibilities in the literature of the 1880s. Portion on James is less substantial than earlier sections.

Edel, Leon. *Henry James.* 5 vols. Philadelphia: J. B. Lippincott, 1953–72. Comprehensive and invaluable life of James that succeeds best on a social level, in detailing his whereabouts and associations. Somewhat weak on the cultural background. Psychological readings and identification of James with his characters tend to be simplistic.

Goode, John, ed. *The Air of Reality: New Essays on Henry James.* London: Metheun & Co., 1972. Anthology of recent essays on the novels by English academics, with the first three essays on *The American, Washington Square,* and *The Bostonians.*

Graham, Kenneth. *Henry James: The Drama of Fulfilment.* New York: Oxford University Press, 1975. James's novels from different periods in the context of desire for personal expansion versus restriction, of struggle for integration between the self and the outer world.

Holland, Laurence Bedwell. *The Expense of Vision: Essays in the Craft of Henry James.* Princeton: Princeton University Press, 1965. Deals with the way in which the visual form of the novels is incorporated into their moral perspective and theme. Largely on the later novels, treated with elaborate reverence, but has opening chapters on *The Portrait.*

Kelley, Cornelia Pulsifer. *The Early Development of Henry James.* Rev. ed. Urbana: University of Illinois Press, 1965. Pioneering, influential work tracing James's development through a closely detailed comparison with his critical writing; entirely on the earlier novels, with *The Portrait* treated too briefly.

Kerr, Howard. *Mediums, and Spirit-Rappers, and Roaring Radicals: Spiritualism in American Literature, 1850–1900.* Urbana: University of Illinois Press, 1972. Informative work treating the

literary-social background of Spiritualism in nineteenth-century
America, with a good section on *The Bostonians.*

Leavis, F. R. *The Great Tradition.* London: George W. Stewart, Inc.,
1948. Opinionated readings by a devout Jamesian endorsing almost all of the earlier novels; particular attention given to *Roderick Hudson, The Europeans, The Portrait,* and *The Bostonians,*
the last two regarded as James's greatest works.

Lebowitz, Naomi. *The Imagination of Loving: Henry James's Legacy
to the Novel.* Detroit: Wayne State University Press, 1965. Study
of the way in which personal relationships, freed of societal or
philosophical attachment, structure the major novels; contains a
lengthy but fuzzy discussion of *The Portrait of a Lady.*

Levy, Leo B. *Versions of Melodrama: A Study of the Fiction and
Drama of Henry James, 1865–1897.* Berkeley: University of Cali-
fornia Press, 1957. Pioneering study of the melodramatic mode
in James, marred by interpretations that are at times heavy-handed.
All of the earlier novels are treated.

Long, Robert Emmet. *The Great Succession: Henry James and the
Legacy of Hawthorne.* Pittsburgh: University of Pittsburgh Press,
1979. Treats James's transformation of Hawthorne's romance
themes and character archetypes into realism, from the early
apprenticeship through *The Bostonians.*

Matthiessen, F. O. *American Renaissance: Art and Expression in the
Age of Emerson and Whitman.* New York: Oxford University
Press, 1941. Major study of nineteenth-century American litera-
ture and culture; concerned with American romanticism in the
age of Emerson, but contains many valuable observations on
James as the heir of the New England tradition.

Maves, Carl. *Sensuous Pessimism: Italy in the Work of Henry James.*
Bloomington: Indiana University Press, 1973. James's romance
with Italy, and developing use of Italy's moral ambivalence in
his works.

McElderry, Bruce R. *Henry James.* New York: Twayne, 1965. Over-
view of James's life and career in a single volume, covering all of
the novels, plays, and stories, with individual works touched on
only very lightly.

Mull, Donald L. *Henry James's "Sublime Economy": Money as Symbolic Center in the Fiction.* Middletown, Conn.: Wesleyan Uni-

186 HENRY JAMES: THE EARLY NOVELS

versity Press, 1973. The role of money, as symbol of freedom and restriction, in selected novels and stories, with a lengthy chapter on *The Portrait of a Lady*.

Poirier, Richard. *The Comic Sense of Henry James: A Study of the Early Novels*. New York: Oxford University Press, 1960. Elegant, accomplished treatment of the earlier novels through *The Portrait of a Lady*. Focuses upon James's comic strategies involving the "freedom" and "fixity" of his characters, with melodramatic expectations raised only to be declined.

Powers, Lyall. *Henry James and the Naturalist Movement*. East Lansing, Michigan State University Press, 1971. James's exposure to French naturalism and application of it in his fiction; particularly relevant to *The Bostonians*.

————, ed. *Henry James's Major Novels*. East Lansing, Mich., 1972. Anthology of good, if very conservatively chosen, essays; earlier novels treated are *Roderick Hudson, The American, The Portrait,* and *The Bostonians*.

Putt, S. Gorley. *Henry James: A Reader's Guide*. Ithaca, New York: Cornell University Press, 1967. Touches deftly on all the novels and tales, arranged by various groupings. Urbanely written, for the general reader.

Samuels, Charles Thomas. *The Ambiguity of Henry James*. Urbana: University of Illinois Press, 1971. Attack on James's major novels having blurred perspective or special advocacies not convincingly validated. Chapters on elements of ambiguity in *The Portrait* and *The Bostonians*.

Stafford, William T., ed. *Perspectives on James's "The Portrait of a Lady": A Collection of Critical Essays*. New York: New York University Press, 1967. Largest of the critical anthologies on *The Portrait*; essays from various periods, supplemented by extensive, annotated bibliography of criticism.

Stone, Donald David. *Novelists in a Changing World: Meredith, James, and the Transformation of English Fiction in the 1880s*. Cambridge, Mass.: Harvard University Press, 1972. Informed, splendidly discriminating account of James and Meredith in the 1880s, illustrating the breakup of the Victorian order. Treats *The Portrait, The Bostonians*, and other early novels.

Tanner, Tony, ed. *Henry James: Modern Judgements*. London: Macmillan, 1968. Collection of essays on James, with generous coverage given to the earlier novels.

Tuttleton, James W., ed. *Henry James: "The American": Critical Edition.* New York: W. W. Norton Co., 1978. Text, with variants, preface to the New York Edition, correspondence surrounding the novel, selection of contemporary English and American reviews, and modern criticism.

Veeder, William. *Henry James—the Lessons of the Master: Popular Fiction and Personal Style in the Nineteenth Century.* Chicago: University of Chicago Press, 1975. Elaborate study of the character types and conventions of popular Victorian fiction affecting James's conception of his novels. Good observations are intermixed with passages of wearisome pedantry. Entirely on the earlier novels.

Ward, J. A. *The Imagination of Disaster: Evil in the Fiction of Henry James.* Lincoln: University of Nebraska Press, 1961. Articulate, sensitively observed study of "evil" in James's fiction, with chapters on *The American* and *The Portrait.*

———. *The Search for Form: Studies in the Structure of James's Fiction.* Chapel Hill: University of North Carolina, 1967. Treats the conflict in James between his allegiances to neoclassical form and to the principle of organic growth of romanticism. Intelligent handling, with chapters on *Watch and Ward* and *The Europeans.*

Winner, Viola Hopkins. *Henry James and the Visual Arts.* Charlottesville: University of Virginia Press, 1970. Close, informed examination of the fine arts in James's novels, with chapters on *Roderick Hudson* and *The Portrait of a Lady.*

Index